77 WAYS
Your Family Can Make a Difference

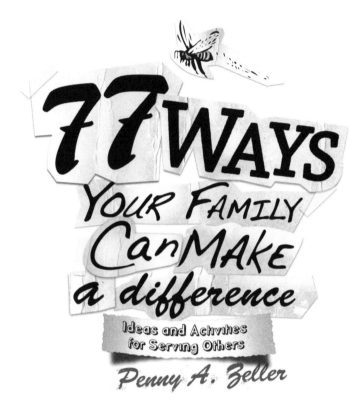

77 WAYS
YOUR FAMILY
Can MAKE
a difference

Ideas and Activities
for Serving Others

Penny A. Zeller

BEACON HILL PRESS
OF KANSAS CITY

Copyright 2008
By Penny A. Zeller and Beacon Hill Press of Kansas City

ISBN 978-0-8341-2370-0

Printed in the
United States of America

Library of Congress Cataloging-in-Publication Data

Zeller, Penny, 1973-
77 ways your family can make a difference : ideas and activities for serving others /
Penny Zeller.
    p. cm.
Includes bibliographical references.
ISBN-13: 978-0-8341-2370-0 (pbk.)
ISBN-10: 0-8341-2370-3 (pbk.)
 1. Family—Religious life. I. Title. II. Title: Seventy-seven ways your family can make a
difference.

BV4526.3.Z45 2008
249—dc22

                                                                    2008014692

10 9 8 7 6 5 4 3 2 1

Contents

Introduction   9

How to Use This Book   11

  1. Design a Bring-It-Back Box   13

  2. Create a Card Ministry   15

  3. Visit a Nursing Home   18

  4. Buy a Week's Worth of Meals   21

  5. Adopt a Missionary   23

  6. Donate Time and Food to the Animal Shelter   25

  7. Spread the Word   27

  8. Send a Pizza   29

  9. Plant Flowers, Trees, or Shrubs   31

 10. Plan a Birthday Party   34

 11. Make a Book   36

 12. Donate Home Furnishings   38

 13. Project: Compassion   40

 14. Invite and Deliver!   42

 15. Hope for the Hospitalized   43

 16. Say Thank You   45

 17. Provide Seasonal Cheer   47

 18. Volunteer Your Time to Babysit   49

 19. Surviving with a Survival Kit   51

 20. Become a Taxi Service   53

 21. Remember Those in Distant Places   55

 22. Purchase Diapers   58

 23. Purchase Small Gifts   60

 24. File Adoption Papers   62

 25. Assist with Vehicle Maintenance   64

 26. Remember Your Sisters and Brothers in Christ   66

 27. Offer to Assist with Clutter Control   68

 28. Support a Worthy Cause   70

 29. Listen   73

 30. Help with Heating Bills   75

31.	Found a Lending Library	77
32.	Visit a Homeless Shelter	79
33.	Send Flowers	81
34.	Give a Bible	83
35.	Pound the Pavement	84
36.	Become a Fundraiser Organizer	85
37.	Take Part in Ministry Outreach	87
38.	Create a Movie or Game Night	90
39.	Pray Without Ceasing	92
40.	Help a Single Mom	95
41.	Celebrate the Christmas Season	97
42.	Beautify Our Surroundings	100
43.	Smile	102
44.	Donate Your Time	103
45.	Bake Treats	105
46.	Host a Garage Sale	107
47.	Plan a Spa Day	109
48.	Plant a Garden	111
49.	Provide an After-School Alternative for a Latchkey Kid	113
50.	Give a Handout	114
51.	Sponsor a Child from Another Country	116
52.	Encourage a Laugh	118
53.	Have a Jammie Day	119
54.	Volunteer as a Tutor	121
55.	Make Beautiful Music	123
56.	Share the Gospel	125
57.	Sew Blankets	127
58.	Give Some Relief Time	129
59.	Plan a GTYC Day	131
60.	Welcome New Neighbors	133
61.	Decorate with Love!	135
62.	Remember Our Soldiers and Their Families	138
63.	Think of Your Own Family Members	142
64.	Create a Bike Ministry	145

65. Extend an Invitation   147
66. Make Meals   149
67. Provide Daily Inspiration and Encouragement   151
68. Host a Party   153
69. Make a Run for It   156
70. Be a Job Scout   158
71. Provide Gift Packs   160
72. Furnish Winter Clothing   162
73. Host a Block Party   164
74. Make Your Voice Count   166
75. Share a Story   168
76. Make It a Birthday to Remember   170
77. Perform a Random Act of Kindness   172
Templates   175
Notes   189

Introduction

A little girl knelt at the edge of her bed and prayed for each member of her family. She then asked God to heal the owie she received while riding her bike. With her head bowed and her eyes closed, she finished her prayer, saying, "And, Lord, please help us find someone to bless tomorrow."

In this world of chaos and busyness, it takes only a moment to bless someone's day. Thoughtful things we can do for one another can really make a difference. Because of this, it's important to teach our children the power that helping others can have. Involving the entire family will teach children to develop a mind-set of serving others as they grow into adulthood. Serving others as a family project has the reward of helping others, and it creates multiple benefits—to those inside the family unit and also to other individuals in need.

Just as the Lord said, we're to treat others the way we would want to be treated and to love our neighbor just as ourselves. What better way for children to understand this principle than to teach them to serve others? And what better way than to model as parents? *77 Ways Your Family Can Make a Difference* provides the platform for doing just that. By using this book as a learning tool, your family will reap many benefits. This book does the following:

- It teaches children to care about and serve others—a valuable lesson that lasts their entire lives.
- It gives families a chance to witness to others.
- Unlike some books that are set aside when the reading is finished, *77 Ways Your Family Can Make a Difference* can be used time and time again.
- Many of the suggestions in the book have no extra expenses.

- It opens up many Bible verses for discussion.
- It helps promote family unity.
- Each suggestion includes an interactive "Up for Discussion" section. This allows children to discuss the importance and the effect of each activity and correlate it to God's Word.

Encourage your family not only to take part in these activities but also to develop a mind-set of servanthood that can, in turn, be passed on to their own children. Put a smile on someone's face—you *can* make a difference!

How to Use This Book

This hands-on book has a collection of 77 suggestions that are written for you—parents, grandparents, youth leaders, and teachers. Such suggestions will assist you in involving your families, youth group, and students in the important and life-changing act of serving others.

Some of the suggestions in this book are designed for family members and friends as recipients, while other suggestions are designed for complete strangers. Regardless of which suggestions you choose to undertake, be sure to pray about each activity, and ask God to bless the people you serve.

You'll note that some of the projects require heavy involvement, while others are very simple. Keep in mind that even simple acts of kindness make a difference.

After each activity is an "Up For Discussion" section. This section is written directly to your children, youth group, and students. The questions and comments within this section are directed and designed for them to answer after your family or youth group has completed the project. The questions help them look deeper into the reasons behind each activity. Many correlate the activity to a particular Bible verse or Bible story. Feel free to add questions and comments of your own during this critical time of sharing, learning, and understanding God's desire for us to serve Him and others.

At the end of each activity is a Bible verse. Discuss this verse with your children and how it applies to their lives, serving others, and living the life God designed for them. You may also wish to have your children memorize the verse. By doing so, they'll be able to more readily call upon the Word of the Lord throughout their lives.

During each of these projects, may you and those you involve in each activity "serve wholeheartedly, as if you were serving the Lord, not men" (Eph. 6:7).

1. Design a Bring-It-Back Box

Sometimes we take family vacations for granted. The pleasure of climbing into the car and escaping for a while is always an option. However, there are many people who, due to health, financial, or other reasons, don't have the privilege of taking short jaunts or extended vacations. Why not bring a vacation to them by creating a Bring-It-Back-Box?

A Bring-It-Back-Box can be made from a cardboard box or plastic container with a lid. A wooden box put together as a family project can be even more creative. Using craft supplies such as paints, crayons, and stickers, spend an evening as a family decorating the box.

Whenever your family takes a vacation, whether to the mountains, the beach, the zoo, or to visit a relative in another state, make it a point to collect mementos from your trip. Place these mementos in your homemade box, and when you've collected quite a few items, give to someone who may never be able to travel to those places. Remember: you don't have to travel far to find a treasure for your Bring-It-Back-Box. Some suggestions for ideas are as follows:

- A pinecone or pretty rock from your camping trip.
- A seashell or sand dollar from the beach.
- A small stuffed animal from the zoo gift shop.
- A beautiful pressed flower from Grandma's yard.
- A drawing of the butterflies at the butterfly farm you visited.
- A dried cattail, interesting leaf, or feather from a family walk.
- A postcard from your trip to another state.

- A coin from that far-off country your family traveled to.
- A picture of your family from an exciting adventure at the aquarium.

To experience this activity even more fully, collect duplicates of the items that your family places in the Bring-It-Back-Box and use them for your family's memory box!

Up for Discussion

Why would creating a Bring-It-Back-Box provide cheer for someone unable to travel? Would that person enjoy receiving a token from one of your trips? Can you think of any other items you could add to his or her box?

So many items that can be used for the Bring-It-Back-Box are those found in nature. God created nature for us to enjoy. Any object found in nature is the best kind to include!

Challenge your parents or sibling(s) to list how many animals they can think of in one minute. How many did you come up with? Why do you think God chose to make so many different types of animals? Why is it important to have an awareness and appreciation for all that God created?

God made the wild animals according to their kinds, the livestock according to their kinds, and all the creatures that move along the ground according to their kinds. And God saw that it was good.

—Gen. 1:25

2. Create a Card Ministry

Greeting cards have been a tradition for over a century, as they convey a message of meaning to someone special. The use of such cards continues to heighten. According to the United States Census Bureau, there are 1.9 billion "Christmas cards sent to friends and loved ones every year, making Christmas the largest card-sending occasion in the United States. The second largest is Valentine's Day, with approximately 192 million cards being given."[1]

Though many cards are sent during Christmas and Valentine's Day, your family doesn't have to wait until, or limit themselves to, those holidays before sending a greeting card. Why not send cards for other reasons, or for no reason at all?

Purchase cards that can be sent for a variety of occasions. Start your collection by purchasing cards that say "thank you," "get well," and "thinking of you." Also purchase sympathy, birthday, and blank cards.

When you know someone who needs to be cheered up, send a card to brighten his or her day. If you think about someone with whom you haven't connected in a while, send a card to say you're thinking of him or her. Did someone do something nice for your family? Give a thank-you card to show your appreciation.

Your family can also opt to send a card for no special reason. In these days of e-mail and electronic communication, a card sent through the post office can be especially meaningful. For your humorous friends, send a birthday card—even if it's not the recipient's birthday. This is sure to draw a laugh.

A way to make your card ministry more meaningful for

you and for others is to send a homemade card. Homemade cards are fun for children to design, and others see the heartfelt effort behind it. Here are some suggestions for ways to make homemade cards:

- Gather construction paper or card stock to use for the cards. Collect buttons, stickers, foam shapes, puffy paints, puffballs, pictures, crayons, markers, scissors, and glue. Combine these items with your children's artwork for a personalized card.
- Don't limit the artwork to kids—make sure the parents use their artistic abilities as well.
- Add a twist to the card. Have the children cut out pictures of themselves using scissors with decorative edges. Glue the pictures onto the cards so relatives can see the latest family snapshots.
- Design a theme for the cards. For birthday cards, use colored paper and dots from a hole punch to create a three-dimensional picture on the front of the card.
- Make sure everyone signs the cards.
- Don't limit yourself to the regularly observed holidays. Your family can make up its own holidays or send a card for one of the less conventional holidays. Some of the wackier holidays include Bubble Bath Day, Backward Day, Make a Hat Day, and Oatmeal Muffin Day.[2]

The important thing to remember is that no matter what time of year it is, showing others that you're thinking of them can make a small but profound difference in their lives.

Up for Discussion

What type of card did you choose to make? Who was it for? Why did you make it? How will you remember to make your card ministry something that happens on a regular basis?

For future cards, think of someone who may be having a rough day. What type of card would you make for that person? Can you think of someone who has been sick recently or someone who needs a thank-you card? How would you decorate those cards?

Think about the card you made for this activity and about the cards you'll create in the future. Why does God want us to be thoughtful and show compassion to others?

You, O Lord, are a compassionate and gracious God,
slow to anger, abounding in love and faithfulness.
—Ps. 86:15

3. Visit a Nursing Home

By 2000 there were 1,557,800 people 65 years of age and older residing in nursing homes.[3] This is a great number of our loved ones, whom we find it too easy to neglect and forget since they are living out of sight in these facilities. Because of this, many seniors experience loneliness, particularly during the holidays.

As individuals with an abundance of resources, we can utilize those resources to reach out and bring cheer to those in nursing homes. Check with the director of a nursing home in your area and obtain the name of a resident who rarely has visitors throughout the year. Use one or more of the following simple acts of kindness to brighten his or her day:

- Put on a small program. If it's Christmastime, sing Christmas carols or read the Christmas story as a family. Invite all the residents to attend.
- Go shopping. Find an appropriate but special gift for someone in a nursing home. Some suggestions include stamps and stationery (why not offer to write a letter for the resident as well?), fuzzy socks, non-scented lotion, or a pre-paid phone card.
- Visit the person before, after, and during the holidays. It's important to maintain contact several times throughout the year (this activity is not just a one-time event). Encourage your children to periodically mail drawings and letters in between visits.
- Bring your camera. Take a few photos of your family with the resident, and be sure to make copies for him or her. Frame and hang the photos as a reminder that your family is now his or her family.

- Preserve history. Some people wish their life story could be preserved for future generations. Help your child record the life story of the person you chose to visit. This can be accomplished by using a tape recorder, camcorder, camera, or notebook. There are many important events in history, such as the Great Depression and World War II, that have had a tremendous impact on the world. Children can learn a great deal from those who experienced those events firsthand.

A visit to a nursing home presents many teachable moments for children. Compassion tops the list, as well as kindness, thoughtfulness, and thankfulness, especially for those less fortunate. Plus an added bonus—you and your children may even make a new friend.

Up for Discussion

Why would it be important for you to get to know someone who grew up many decades ago? How is his or her life different from yours? Ponder the amazing reality of how God knew which time period we would live in long before we were born.

Before your next visit to the nursing home, prepare a list of questions to interview someone who is now in his or her seventies or eighties about his or her life as a child. Start with questions similar to these:

- What was your favorite game?
- What was your school like?
- What type of gifts did you receive for Christmas?
- Would you rather be a child then or a child growing up now?

Throughout the Bible, God reveals the importance of learning from those who came before us. Consider the priest Eli's influence in Samuel's life. Consider Ruth's devotion to Naomi, her mother-in-law. Think about the life lessons you can learn from your parents, grandparents, and those you visited at the nursing home. Discuss the importance of teaching the younger generation described in Titus 2.

> Rise in the presence of the aged, show respect for the elderly
> and revere your God. I am the LORD.
> —Lev. 19:32

4. Buy a Week's Worth of Meals

Hundreds of families across the country can't afford even the most basic needs—especially food. A good exercise to teach your children about helping others is to buy groceries for a family. Call your local Salvation Army or food bank, and find out the food needs of a family in your area.

When our family embarked on this project, we asked for a family who had the same family makeup as ours (although this is not necessary)—a family with two girls, a mother, and a father. This helped our girls to better identify with the family and to consider how it might feel if we were in a predicament in which we had no food.

Once we had the list of needs, we purchased enough complete meal items for the family to eat for a week. Some ideas:

- Oatmeal, cereal, eggs, pancake mix
- Bread, lunch meat, peanut butter and jelly, macaroni and cheese, tortillas, beans, cheese
- Fresh fruit and vegetables—bananas, apples, carrots, celery, lettuce, potatoes
- Miscellaneous items—hot dogs, chicken nuggets, spaghetti sauce and noodles, meal kits, cake mixes, canned frosting, graham crackers, cheese sticks, granola bars, fruit cups
- Milk, orange juice, and coffee.

Our girls also added a drawing for the daughters of the family, and our entire family delivered the items to the Salvation Army, who in turn delivered the food to the family. One of the highlights of this project is to include some fun and tasty items that, because of their budget, a needy family may not otherwise have a chance to enjoy.

Up for Discussion

A woman once told me that while she was grateful for the local food bank, the only food items donated were the kind that no one else would eat and that few people actually liked to eat. As one who desperately depended on the food bank, this presented a very difficult choice: eat the unpleasant food or continue to be hungry.

Why does it matter? Why is it important that we donate groceries that a needy family would enjoy? How might this change your perspective the next time you donate food items?

Read Matt. 25:40. Why do you think God tells us in His Word that when we do something for someone in need, we're really doing it for Him?

> The King will reply, "I tell you the truth, whatever you did for
> one of the least of these brothers of mine, you did for me."
>
> —Matt. 25:40

5. Adopt a Missionary

Reaching everyone in the world with God's Word is not always an easy task. Missionaries often travel to distant and dangerous locations to do the Lord's work. And those who serve in the United States are not without their challenges as well. In 2000 there were "410,000 missionaries from all branches of Christendom" and "64,000 Protestant missionaries from USA."[4]

Check with your church regarding the missionaries it supports. Choose—"adopt"—a missionary (or a missionary family), and have members of your family write letters of encouragement, letting him or her know of your thoughts and prayers. Ask if there is anything you can send that might help as he or she serves the Lord.

Our family's missionary friends and pen pals are serving in Alaska. Their needs have been various: clothing for the people on their mission field and for their own family, Christian books and videos, cake mixes for their Sunday community get-togethers, and so on.

A missionary and her husband from Tibet recently spoke to our women's Bible study group, informing us that the people in the village where they serve love coffee and ranch dressing. She also mentioned that she would appreciate donations of wholesome children's videos for her sons.

Find out what things your adopted missionary family needs. You would be surprised at just how little it takes to help them serve.

Adopting a missionary is only one way we help those God has called to spread the gospel. In addition, this activity promotes God's instruction that we are to reach everyone throughout the world with His Word.

Up for Discussion

Why do you think it's important that people become missionaries? Do you think missionaries should serve only in faraway countries, or do you believe a missionary can serve here in the United States as well? Why or why not? What are some difficulties that a missionary's child may face? What could you do to assist him or her with those difficulties? Can you be a missionary in your own hometown? How?

Discuss Rom. 14:11. What does this verse mean? How does it affect us, even those who haven't accepted Christ as their Savior?

> *"As surely as I live," says the Lord, "every knee will bow before me;*
> *every tongue will confess to God."*
> —Rom. 14:11

6. Donate Time and Food to the Animal Shelter

Animal shelters care for between 6 and 8 million dogs and cats every year in the United States.[5] This is a large amount of needy animals, many that won't receive proper attention because there aren't enough resources available.

Take a moment to help some of God's most loving creatures. Begin by calling your local animal shelter. Find out what types of food the shelter needs—bags of dry dog food, cans of cat food, and so on. Ask if your family can bring food to the shelter.

Take a peek inside an animal shelter, and you'll find it's evident many of these animals would love some attention, if only for a short time. Your family may choose instead (or in addition to a food donation) to assist in walking the dogs one day a week for a month or on a one-time basis.

Why not offer to start an adoption drive for the animals in your local shelter? Ask the staff of the shelter if your family can make and display posters and flyers regarding the adoption drive. Use the artistic skills of family members to draw profiles of the dogs and cats available for adoption. Or if there's a budding photographer in the family, enlist his or her talents to take photos of the animals waiting for a home. Another idea is to have the computer whiz in your family create flyers on the computer. Take a family walk through town to distribute the flyers. In this way your entire family can be involved in pairing pets with new owners.

Why do you think God put us in charge of the animals? How do you think He would want us to care for pets that have no home? Do you make sure your pet it is fed and has enough water and exercise? Why?

Take a minute to think about the moment when God asked Adam to name each of the creatures He made. Can you imagine Adam's amazement when he saw the different varieties of animals? Try to name some of the especially unique animals that attest to God's incredible imagination.

The wolf will live with the lamb, the leopard will lie down with the goat, the calf and the lion and the yearling together; and a little child will lead them.

—Isa. 11:6

7. Spread the Word

The United States Postal Service handles billions of pieces of mail each year. Mail is a good way to send messages. Want your family to help spread the word of God's love? Why not take advantage of the way that huge numbers of mail are seen by many eyes each day?

Find meaningful and encouraging Scripture verses. Have your children write the verses on the back flap of the envelope of bills, packages, letters, and other correspondence. Be sure the verses are written in small print and are not covering the addresses. (That's why the backside works best.) My grandma first started this trend in our family. Since she lives in another state, we receive a lot of mail from her. On each item she mails to us—whether it is a letter or a package—she always includes a Bible verse.

Need some ideas for verses? Write down several on a master list. Keep it handy for future reference. Here are some good ones to get you started:

- Ps. 25:4
- Ps. 136:1
- Ps. 139:4
- Prov. 4:23
- Matt. 17:20
- John 3:16
- Phil. 4:8
- Heb. 11:3

A number of other verses can be used for this activity. Encourage your children to add them to the list above.

Take this idea further by having your children write "God loves you" or "Jesus loves you" on each letter or package they mail to their friends and relatives. Put these phrases on the inside of the letter or package, as opposed to the outside. Our oldest daughter began this habit, and now there isn't a letter or a thank-you note that leaves this house without her trademark words telling of Christ's love!

When we recently put together a box of items for some foster children, the items placed at the top of the box were the letters from our daughters declaring God's love for them. Such projects encourage children to be bold in their faith.

Up for Discussion

Which verses did you choose for this project? How does writing scripture on envelopes and packages spread the gospel? Why is sharing the gospel important? How many people do you think will see the verses? How might this help someone who is curious about God?

Read Rom. 1:16. Why should we not be ashamed of the gospel? How has this activity confirmed the fact that your family is not ashamed? Have you ever been embarrassed to be a Christian? What prayer can you pray asking God to help you spread His Word?

I am not ashamed of the gospel, because it is the power of God for the salvation of everyone who believes: first for the Jew, then for the Gentile.

—Rom. 1:16

8. Send a Pizza

Did you know that October is National Pizza Month? Everyone should be able to enjoy this tasty treat. Yet some cannot. Since shut-in folks are unable to go anywhere, having a pre-paid pizza delivered to their door would be a special treat. Call someone your family knows who can't go out for pizza themselves. Be sure to find out their favorite kind (first find out about any food allergies), and have it delivered to their house.

Or, to make the pizza delivery extra-special, have a family night by making a homemade pizza and hand-delivering it. You can opt to make a homemade crust or buy an already-prepared one. Top the pizza with sauce, cheese, and the recipient's favorite toppings. For a single recipient, smaller-sized pizzas work well.

Up for Discussion

Who did your family send a pizza to? Why? How can something as ordinary as a pizza make a difference in someone's life?

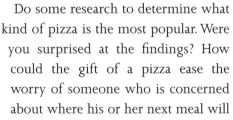

Do some research to determine what kind of pizza is the most popular. Were you surprised at the findings? How could the gift of a pizza ease the worry of someone who is concerned about where his or her next meal will come from?

Read Gal. 6:9. Why should we continue doing kind things for others? Why should acts of thoughtfulness be done more than just once?

Let us not become weary in doing good, for at the proper time
we will reap a harvest if we do not give up.

—Gal. 6:9

9. Plant Flowers, Trees, or Shrubs

Nothing says summer like a garden of beautiful flowers or a shady tree. But to some, planting a garden can be a daunting task. Offer to do the planting for a friend or neighbor. Not only will this brighten his or her day, but digging in the dirt is also a fun family undertaking. Below are some different ways to accomplish this project.

- Your family may opt to plant a garden or a pot of flowers. Determine if the recipient would enjoy perennial plants (those that will return year after year), or if he or she prefers annual plants (those that live only for one season). If annuals, remind the person that these flowers may be planted in a pot and brought in to the house during the cold winter months. If properly cared for in a warm environment, the plants will bloom again the following year. Some examples of perennial flowers include creeping phlox, peonies, perennial geraniums, and day-lilies. Examples of annuals include alyssum, pansies, begonias, and zinnias.

- Another way to deliver the cheer of flowers is to do so around Easter. Our family poked holes in the bottom of small metal watering cans and used a plastic lid for water drainage. Small pots and planters will work as well. We planted flowers in the watering cans, and our girls decorated the outside with Bible verses, such as "He has risen" (Matt. 28:6). We delivered several to our friends, even those who aren't Christians. Some ideas for the watering can flowers include petunias, violets, lilies, daisies, and marigolds.

- Shrubs can be a nice addition to any yard. Some examples of shrubs: potentilla, spiraea, variegated weigela, burning bush, and angel's trumpet.
- Why not use a tree as a way to make a difference? Use the Internet for research or check with your local nursery for the types of trees that grow well in your area. Again, obtain permission before digging, and check with utility companies for the location of underground lines.

Has someone you know recently lost a friend or loved one? Ask if you can plant a tree in that person's memory. The birth of a child or grandchild can also be celebrated by planting a tree. Would a tree be a perfect birthday gift for someone? Tree ideas include willows, maples, pine trees, aspen, and ash trees.

Whether you choose flowers, shrubs, or trees, use the vegetation of God's creation to make a difference in someone's life!

Up for Discussion

What kind of response did you receive after giving a plant to someone? How could a plant teach someone about God's creation? How might a plant bearing the phrase "He has risen" open up a conversation with a neighbor who is curious about what Jesus did for us? What other Bible verses would be good to write on the container?

Have you ever noticed that we attempt to duplicate the wonderful smells of flowers and pine trees but can never quite achieve matching the scent of the real thing? How might the mere scent of flowers and trees brighten someone's day? How can the vivid colors of plants bring joy to someone? How might the wind that blows through the tree you just planted remind someone of God's presence?

Read Ps. 103:15. Discuss how, like that of the grass and

flowers, our time on earth is short. How should this make a difference in the way we spend our time?

As for man, his days are like grass, he flourishes like a flower of the field.
—Ps. 103:15

10. Plan a Birthday Party

Every day is someone's birthday, and many people enjoy having some type of celebration on that day. However, some people spend their birthdays alone and in silence.

Spread some birthday cheer by planning a group birthday party for those who usually spend their birthdays alone. Begin by locating a nursing home, an assisted-living home, a group home for the disabled, or a home for troubled youth. Arrange for your family to come once a month (or quarterly) with some goodies for all the residents. Celebrate by singing "Happy Birthday to You" to residents who have birthdays in each given month. Be sure to obtain the number of birthday participants beforehand, and provide a treat for every resident. (Take sugar-free treats as an alternative for those who can't have sugar.) Some ideas for birthday treats:

- Sugar cookies decorated with frosting and sprinkles.
- Homemade fudge individually wrapped in decorative wrap.
- Chocolate-and-vanilla marbled cupcakes, each with a candle.
- Frosted mini-cupcakes with a heart candy on the top.

Take this activity a step further for enjoyment, and supply birthday hats and party blowers for each participant. For those who have birthdays in a given month, make and distribute birthday ID cards, such as the one found in the templates section of this book (these can be easily typed on cardstock and cut apart). For a homemade look, have the children add birthday stickers or drawings of birthday cakes to the cards. Laminate them to ensure that they will last a good while.

When several friends joined our efforts to provide a birthday party at an assisted-living home, we also purchased a pair of socks for each person celebrating a birthday, wrapped them, and handed them out during the ceremony. As a reminder of the party, we also took a group photo of those celebrating a birthday during that month. We later framed and delivered it to the assisted-living home, where it was displayed.

No matter what type of party you plan to throw for the group birthday party, have all the family members combine their skills and talents for the event. Can your son recite a poem he learned in school? Those at the birthday party would love to hear it. Can your daughter rival Beethoven on the piano? Provide a concert for the party. Can you decorate a cake? Bake one for the party. Have everyone in the family help decorate the cake, each member decorating his or her own portion any way he or she wishes. Is your husband an amateur movie producer? Ask him to film the party and provide the facility with a tape or DVD of the event. Have friends who would love to join in? Invite them. Make this a birthday party like none other!

Up for Discussion

How did acknowledging the birthday of someone brighten his or her day? What other activities could your family include for future group birthday parties?

Consider how people in the Old Testament lived longer than we do today. For example, Methuselah (Noah's grandfather) lived to the ripe old age of 969, while Noah lived to be 950. Abraham lived 175 years, and Moses lived to be 120. Why do you think this was?

Read Ps. 22:10. How does this verse provide you with comfort? Think about how God never changes but remains constant throughout the many births and deaths that occur each day.

From birth I was cast upon you; from my mother's womb you have been my God.

—Ps. 22:10

11. Make a Book

Some activities are meaningful but don't last. A way to make a difference in a meaningful *and* lasting way is to make a book.

A few years ago at our family's Thanksgiving get-together, my sister Becky came up with an excellent idea—she made books for each member of the family. These were not ordinary books—they were homemade books that we titled *We Are Thankful to God for [insert name of family member] Because* . . . Each member of the family had his or her own book with his or her name filled in each blank of the book.

As each person arrived at the get-together, he or she was asked to write in the books of others, detailing reasons to be thankful for each particular family member. Even my niece, Ally, who was five at the time, participated. She wrote in my book, "I am blessed because of Aunt Penny's macaroni and cheese."

These books are easy for your family to make for each other and are a sentimental keepsake. Begin by deciding what type of book your family will create. Becky cut square pieces of heavy-duty colored paper and stapled several pieces together. The title was written on the cover. Your family may choose to use tablets or inexpensive journals rather than making the books. Children can decorate the covers or interiors with drawings, poems, or stickers.

Place each book on the table so that when guests arrive, they are able to write in each book. Encourage children to participate and write in the books. Be sure to put a date on the back cover to remember the occasion in the future. The same books may also be used from year to year, with dates accompanying each occasion. These books can also be made as birthday gifts or for no holiday in particular.

Whatever the time of year, this is an inspiring idea that allows the family to highlight the best qualities in everyone and focus on what's important—"The LORD does not look at the things man looks at. Man looks at the outward appearance, but the LORD looks at the heart" (1 Sam. 16:7).

Up for Discussion

Consider 1 Sam. 16:7. Why is God's idea of an important focus better than the world's idea of an important focus? James 3 states, "The tongue also is a fire, a world of evil among the parts of the body . . . but no man can tame the tongue" (vv. 6, 8). How can something so small and seemingly innocent as the tongue be an evil part of the body that cannot be tamed? Why do you think God discusses the importance of using our tongues to speak kindness to others? How is a kind word or a kind note in keeping with this verse?

Read Eph. 4:29. Why should we strive to say things that encourage others rather than things that can hurt someone? How does this apply to writing words and notes that are beneficial to others instead of notes that speak unkindly about someone?

> Do not let any unwholesome talk come out of your mouths,
> but only what is helpful for building others up according to their needs,
> that it may benefit those who listen.
> —Eph. 4:29

12. Donate Home Furnishings

Every day and in every part of the country, people are moving into new homes. Perhaps they're transitioning from a group home, a homeless shelter, or aging out of foster care. Whatever the reason for beginning a new life in a home of their own, they have a definite need for household items.

But those who need household items can't always afford them. To help remedy this, arrange for a group of families or for your church to donate home furnishings to those in need. Check to see if you have anything in duplicate. Many households have several television sets, extra mattresses, and unused furniture. Such items could provide comfort and make a huge difference in the life of someone who has very little. "Thin out" your belongings, and donate your duplicates to this worthy cause.

Inexpensive household items can also be purchased for donation. Some ideas:

- Bath or dish towels
- Kitchen items (spatulas, measuring cups, salt and pepper shakers, and so on)
- Silverware
- Potholders
- Cookbooks
- Bathroom or dish soap
- Sheets or blankets

Up for Discussion

Many of us take for granted that when we open the silverware drawer, there's a fork or a spoon in it ready to be used. Warm blankets on our beds during a cold winter go unappreciated, as do the dining room chairs and the pots and pans we use to cook dinner every night. What other household items might we take for granted that someone else could use?

Who helped you donate items for others? How did you arrange this effort? How do you think everyone felt as he or she participated in this activity?

Read 1 John 3:17. How does showing compassion for others and sharing with them indicate the love of God within you?

If anyone has material possessions and sees his brother in need but has no pity on him, how can the love of God be in him?
—1 John 3:17

13. Project: Compassion

While many people have various material needs, some just need an extra thought or prayer because of a hurt in their life. Have your family make a difference by offering condolences of compassion and sympathy for those in painful situations.

When our relatives lost their newborn infant to a fatal birth defect, we decided to gather our friends to provide emotional support. We sent out e-mails and made phone calls, asking our friends if they would be willing to write a prayer, a card, or a short condolence for our relatives. Although none of these friends knew our relatives (they lived over 650 miles away), they were willing to heed our request. We printed out the e-mails and gathered the cards and mailed them in a huge envelope to our relatives. What a blessing for our relatives to know that people they had never met were caring about them and praying for them during their time of sorrow!

Something important to remember: don't forget about those you helped for this activity. So many times our inclination is to help out once—and then go about life and forget. Follow-up is critical. Remember to call or write a second card, and most importantly, consistently keep those individuals in your prayers. The initial hurt or shock may have passed, but their pain still exists.

Up for Discussion

How did this activity help someone in his or her time of sadness? What was the response of those you asked to participate? What was the response of the recipient?

By asking for notes of condolence, people are working together as a group, showing their love for God and their concern for their neighbor. How does including others in an activity like this build fellowship? Why do you think God wants us to have fellowship?

When you contacted others about their involvement in this project, how were you able to use scripture or prayer as a tool? Why is this important? Read Heb. 10:24-25. Why do you think it's important to "spur one another on toward love and good deeds"? Discuss the importance of encouraging others.

Read the account of Noah in Gen. 6—9. In chapter 6 we read,

> The LORD was grieved that he had made man on the earth, and his heart was filled with pain. So the LORD said, "I will wipe mankind, whom I have created, from the face of the earth—men and animals, and creatures that move along the ground, and birds of the air—for I am grieved that I have made them." But Noah found favor in the eyes of the LORD (vv. 6-8).

Noah and his wife, sons, and their wives were the only people on board the ark—and the only humans who survived the Great Flood. How do you think Noah and his family encouraged each other during this difficult time? Why do you think this encouragement was critical, especially during a time when so many of their friends and acquaintances would soon perish? How was the fellowship among Noah's family members during their time on the ark? Was it comforting to each family member?

Let us consider how we may spur one another on toward love and good deeds. Let us not give up meeting together, as some are in the habit of doing, but let us encourage one another—and all the more as you see the Day approaching.
—Heb. 10:24-25

14. Invite and Deliver!

It's amazing how willing people can be to attend church or a Bible study when they have the opportunity to go with someone rather than to go alone. Knowing this, invite someone to church or a Bible study, and be sure to offer a ride as well. Let your children create an invitation for your intended guest. A good example is found in the templates section of the book (this same idea can be used for any church function, including a Bible study or Sunday School). Make it a family affair, and encourage your guest to accompany your family to church every Sunday.

Remember that some individuals may decline an invitation to a Bible study if they don't have the funds to purchase the accompanying book or materials. Assure your guest that he or she will not have to pay anything, as you'll find a way through donations or scholarships to provide the book for him or her.

Up for Discussion

What was the response of the person you invited to church? How many friends can you list who don't go to church? Why do you think attending church is important? Is your youth group or Sunday School class planning a special function to which you could invite a friend or a neighbor? Why is spending time in prayer necessary before extending an invitation like this one?

Read Josh. 24:15. Why is it important that those in your home serve the Lord? In what ways can you serve Him?

> As for me and my household, we will serve the LORD.
> —Josh. 24:15

15. Hope for the Hospitalized

Cancer is only one of the diseases that run rampant through society. It puts millions in the hospital every year, and that's only in North America. Because of the increasing amount of hospitalizations—many that are without hope— you and your family can choose to spread a smile or a word of care to those inflicted with illnesses.

Connect with your pastor and find a way for your family to help those in the hospital. You should be willing to help both those who have no one to visit with them and those who do not have a church home. Many times those with illnesses long for a caring person to talk to. Providing a listening ear and an encouraging smile allows those individuals to hope for recovery. You can also provide hope for those with terminal illnesses by sharing the plan of salvation (if they're receptive to hearing it). Inquire at your local Christian bookstore regarding some appropriate books to use, and be sure to provide a Bible for the individual you're visiting.

Of all the ways your family can make a difference, the gift of time is the most important. To be able to sit with someone, especially someone with an illness, is a treasure that means more than your family will ever realize.

Up for Discussion

Discuss the response you received from the person you visited. Were you able to discuss the gift of salvation? Why was this a critical conversation to have?

2 Peter 3:8-9 states, "With the LORD a day is like a thousand years, and a thousand years are like a day. The LORD is not slow

in keeping his promise, as some understand slowness. He is patient with you, not wanting anyone to perish, but everyone to come to repentance." Discuss how God's timing is different from our timing. How could a half hour of your time mean 24 hours to someone who is in need of a listening ear and a caring heart? How can the gift of time be the most important gift of all? How do you feel when someone spends time with you?

Think about the way that God gives people sufficient time to come to know Him so that no one perishes. What can this mean for someone with a terminal illness?

Read 1 Cor. 9:23. What do you think Paul means when he talks of doing something "for the sake of the gospel"? How does doing something because you want credit or glory from those around you negate the importance of this verse and the kind activity you undertook?

I do all this for the sake of the gospel, that I may share in its blessings.
—1 Cor. 9:23

16. Say Thank You

How often are kind things done for us, yet we forget to say thank you? In our often hurried society, these two small words—which have such a big impact—are not used nearly enough. Encourage your family to spend a day saying thank you to anyone who does something nice or provides a service. For example, say thank you—

- To the grocery clerk who bags your groceries and helps you carry them to your vehicle.
- To the school lunch lady who serves your children lunch.
- To your children's teachers.
- To the person who holds a door open for you.
- With a wave, to the stranger who allows you to go first at a four-way-stop or stops so you can cross the street.
- To the one at the fast-food restaurant who hands you your lunch.
- To the cashier at the restaurant who counts out your change.
- To the librarian who checks your books out to you.

Take this appreciation to an even higher level—do you have food allergies that required a restaurant to prepare a special meal for you? Did a business go out of its way to locate and order a product you were looking for? Did someone donate items for your children's school project? You can also write a letter to the editor of your local newspaper explaining any gratitude you wish to extend.

Up for Discussion

Why is saying thank you so important? Make a list of those who have done nice things for you today. How can you thank them? What about people you don't know, like restaurant workers or salesclerks? Could you complete a survey card, detailing their kind service? How could this positive review help their careers and their lives?

Hebrews 12:28-29 states, "Since we are receiving a kingdom that cannot be shaken, let us be thankful, and so worship God acceptably with reverence and awe, for our 'God is a consuming fire.'" Discuss how God appreciates that we continue to praise and say thank you for all He has given us. Why is praising Him a necessary part of knowing Him?

Read Matt. 7:12. If everyone tried to apply this verse in his or her daily activities, would the world be a different place? How so?

> In everything, do to others what you would have them do to you,
> for this sums up the Law and the Prophets.
> —Matt. 7:12

17. Provide Seasonal Cheer

Each new season brings a new set of holidays, colors, and weather, among many other things. Use each season for inspiration as you provide something new and thoughtful for a friend or loved one.

- During the spring, offer to walk your neighbor's dog. Dogs are very popular—there are millions in the United States alone.
- During the summer, mow your neighbor's or friend's lawn. He or she will be so appreciative to come home to a nicely mowed lawn! Offer to water someone's flowers, trees, and lawn while he or she is away on vacation.
- During the fall, rake leaves for someone. Let the kids jump in the piles before bagging up the leaves.
- During the winter, shovel the sidewalk of your neighbor down the street. It's especially fun to shovel the walkway of someone who is at work all day. Arriving home after the snowstorm, your neighbor will be surprised to see that his or her driveway is already cleared.

Speaking of snow, did you know that on February 2, 2004, students, parents, and teachers from 60 schools in the London, Ontario, District Catholic School Board made 15,851 snow angels simultaneously?[6] How much fun that would be! Use the time with your children to make snow angels in your own yard.

Discuss which activity was the most meaningful to you. Which do you think was the most meaningful for the recipient? Which activity did you enjoy the most? What other types of seasonal kindness can you think of that would show kindness?

Read Lev. 19:18. Why do you think the second greatest command is to love your neighbor? Discuss why a neighbor is not just someone who lives in the house next to you.

Love your neighbor as yourself.

—Lev. 19:18

18. Volunteer Your Time to Babysit

Motherhood can be a very time-consuming job. Many mothers take their children to a mothers' group, such as MOPS (Mothers of Preschoolers), where volunteers babysit their children while the mothers have a day of fun or take a day for themselves. In fact, there are more than 3,900 MOPS groups meeting across the United States and in 35 countries around the world.[7]

The large amount of groups like MOPS only means a large need for volunteer babysitters. Encourage your teenagers to volunteer their time at a local mothers' group. This is an excellent opportunity for teens who wish to serve God in a ministry that is sometimes overlooked. Locate a local group, and inquire about their babysitting needs and their requirements for volunteering. As with any babysitting job, be sure your teenagers brush up on important items such as CPR, the Heimlich maneuver, and games for amusing toddlers. Stress to them the importance of arriving on time and offering to stay late if necessary.

Another way to volunteer is in the church nursery or as an assistant for Sunday School, children's church, or Vacation Bible School. As a volunteer for our children's church and Vacation Bible School, I know that the assistance I received from the junior high and high school helpers was invaluable, and it permitted me to be a more effective teacher.

The choices for volunteering as a babysitter are endless. But what better way for your teens to teach young ones about God?

How was offering to babysit for a mothers' group or in your church nursery especially beneficial to the parents whose children you babysat? What types of activities did you include for the children you babysat?

How might God use you to teach a younger child about God's love? Read Matt. 19:14. Why do you think Jesus felt so strongly about making time for the little children? Why do you think it's critical to teach children about Jesus and His love for them?

> Jesus said, "Let the little children come to me, and do not hinder them,
> for the kingdom of heaven belongs to such as these."
> —Matt. 19:14

19. Surviving with a Survival Kit

Family vacations can be exciting, adventurous, and fun. They can also be exhausting and tiresome. You may feel you need a kit just to survive.

If a family you know is taking a vacation, create a travel survival kit for them, providing necessary items to help their trip go smoothly. Purchase a large, plain tote bag and some puff paints. Have a family night and decorate the bag, painting the words "Travel Survival Kit for the [insert family's last name here] Family" on it. Purchase the following items to be placed in the kit:

- A first-aid kit
- Hand wipes
- Treats, such as beef jerky, granola bars, cheese and crackers, and dried fruit
- A case of bottled water
- Books, including a Bible
- Tablets and pencils (crayons melt in the car, so avoid including them)
- Audio CDs, such as Focus on the Family's *Adventures in Odyssey*
- Mini-travel games. In addition to store-bought games, encourage your children to design and develop their own games for the traveling family
- A comfy pillow
- A map
- A gas card
- Discount coupons for meals or amusement parks near their destination (these can often be found online)

- A list of important phone numbers they can contact in case of an emergency
- Postcards and stamps for them to mail along the way
- Disposable camera

Up for Discussion

What other items did you think to include in the survival kit? What was the response of the family when they received their travel survival kit?

Read Matt. 6:26. How does the survival of wild birds depend on God's care? How do baby humans and baby animals depend on their parents for survival? How are sick people dependent on caregivers and medication for their survival? In a difficult situation, how can prayer make a difference for our survival? Discuss how our eternal survival depends on knowing God.

Look at the birds of the air; they do not sow or reap or store away in barns, and yet your heavenly Father feeds them. Are you not much more valuable than they?

—Matt. 6:26

20. Become a Taxi Service

Many people can't drive for one reason or another. Some don't have a driver's license; some are affected by old age. Others have an illness or a physical handicap that prevents them from driving. And others simply can't afford a car.

Because of these restrictions, transportation is an issue. Many individuals who can't drive are always in need of a ride to or from an important appointment, church, or various errands, such as going to the grocery store.

If you don't already know anyone who is in need of transportation assistance, contact your church or a local assisted-living facility, and obtain the name of someone who has this need. Use your car for transportation and your children as conversationalists.

Other suggestions for ways to help include the following:

- Drive a sick patient to a doctor's appointment. Help those with illnesses, such as cancer or MS, keep their appointments. Not only do you provide transportation, but you also offer a caring shoulder if needed.
- Take your elderly friend to her beauty parlor appointment. Make a date of it, and have your hair done at the same time.
- Reunite a grandparent with his or her grandchildren. Take someone to watch a grandchild play in a sports game or take part in a school performance.
- Help a shut-in. Call the person to see if he or she needs any groceries delivered. Or perhaps the shut-in wants a few library books to read or audiotapes to listen to.

Unless we find ourselves in that very situation, those of us with a vehicle and a driver's license may never know the hardship of not having a means of transportation. Lend your time and your "taxi service" to someone who doesn't have his or her own transportation, and you'll be providing the person with the blessing of freedom.

Up for Discussion

Who did you choose to help with your taxi service? What was your role in providing it?

Consider the story of the paralyzed man in Mark 2. The man was carried by four of his friends to see Jesus. "Since they could not get him to Jesus because of the crowd, they made an opening in the roof above Jesus and, after digging through it, lowered the mat the paralyzed man was lying on" (v. 4). Ponder how the paralyzed man's friends provided transportation for him since he could not walk himself. Discuss how your own offer of transportation in this activity can be critical to the person who would otherwise not have a means of travel.

*In everything I did, I showed you that by this kind of hard work we must
help the weak, remembering the words the Lord Jesus himself said:
"It is more blessed to give than to receive."*
—Acts 20:35

21. Remember Those in Distant Places

In a society in which many families no longer live in the same town or the same state as their relatives, it's important to stay in touch with those close to our hearts, even when they are far from our homes. There are a number of ways that children of all ages can make family members across the miles feel loved and remembered.

- Have your children draw or paint pictures of what they are currently doing in their lives. For example, if your daughter is taking ballet, have her draw a picture of what she has learned in class. Decorate and address the envelope as well, mailing it to her out-of-state grandparent.

- Make place mats. These are the perfect, lasting gifts. Have your children design place mats that include drawings, stickers, paintings, Bible verses, and photos. Use these homemade gifts to brighten the days of far-away relatives as they are reminded of your children's love every time they sit down to a meal.

- Create a mystery to solve. Have your children write a letter with a secret message. Paste it securely on a piece of cardboard. Children can then cut the letter into several puzzle pieces. Mail the puzzle with a note asking a cousin in another state to solve the mystery by completing the puzzle.

- Stock up on postcards. Purchase them from your hometown or other towns. Have your children periodically write notes to loved ones on the postcards. They are quick, easy, inexpensive, and fun to receive!

- Write a continuing saga. When my niece and nephews moved to another state, their grandmother was diligent in keeping in touch. She would send them stories with mysteries to solve, having used them as the main characters. She even made personalized t-shirts for them to wear while they were solving the mysteries. Gather your family together and write stories for and about your relatives. Provide a new mystery or story for them each month.
- Need another story idea? Try a "start and finish story." Have your children begin writing a story, which they mail to your relatives. Your relatives add one or two paragraphs, then they return the story. The story continues back and forth, each time increasing in plot, length, and enjoyment until someone declares it finished. Illustrations are also welcome.
- Become a film director. Use the camcorder to film your children putting on a puppet show or sledding down the hill on a cold, snowy day. Be sure to include some footage from previous videos onto the videotape as well. Grandparents will love receiving a film of your children that highlights some special moments from their baby days as well as their present junior-high basketball games.
- Mail little goodies. Our great-grandma sends monthly boxes of goodies to my children that include dollar-store finds, coloring books, interesting newspaper clippings, and comics. My mother-in-law, who lives in another state, regularly mails my husband homemade no-bake cookies (his favorite).

Although they may not live close by, such ideas allow friends and relatives to know that they are a large and important part of your children's lives.

Up for Discussion

Which idea did your family choose for this activity? How did staying in touch in this way provide a way for you to maintain a close relationship with your relatives? Can you think of other activities you could do that would be meaningful? Why is staying in touch important? How can you make sure to stay in touch with your relatives on a regular basis?

Take a moment to think about how God loves us no matter where we live. How might this truth be applied to your relationship with your far-away relatives through the above activities?

> He will be an instrument for noble purposes, made holy,
> useful to the Master and prepared to do any good work.
> —2 Tim. 2:21

22. Purchase Diapers

In January 2007, it was expected that the United States would register an average of one birth every eight seconds.[8] This is a lot of babies—which all require a large number of diapers.

However, not all parents can afford the cost of diapers. Contact your local WIC (Women, Infants, and Children) organization or social service agency, and inquire about their diaper needs. Offer to purchase and drop off a few packages of diapers and baby wipes for a mother who is struggling financially. The agency will be able to distribute the diapers to the mother in need.

There are some agencies, such as the New Hope Center in Crestview Hills, Kentucky, that provide services for unwed and teenage mothers. But no matter the situation of the recipient, there is a constant need for diaper donations.

You could take this activity even further by involving your family and having a diaper-donation week. Ask members of your church, school, and neighborhood to donate packages of diapers that will all be sent to a designated agency.

Up for Discussion

How does providing diapers for a mother's infant make a difference in her life and ease her burden? What are some fundraising activities you and your family could undertake to raise money for diapers and baby wipes? How could this be an ongoing charity to which your family could donate?

Read and explain Col. 3:12. In this activity you are helping to clothe a baby. Describe how this act of kindness correlates to this verse.

Mark 5:36-43 tells of a man named Jairus whose 12-year-old daughter died. Saddened by this, Jairus went to Jesus, hoping He could heal his daughter. Jesus told Jairus, "Don't be afraid; just believe" (v. 36). Later He healed Jairus's daughter.

What do you think Jairus's response was when his daughter was able to walk around after being presumed dead? Why do you think Jesus told Jairus to "just believe"? How does a miracle like this reinforce Jesus' love for children?

Therefore, as God's chosen people, holy and dearly loved, clothe yourselves with compassion, kindness, humility, gentleness and patience.

—Col. 3:12

23. Purchase Small Gifts

In 2002 more than 6.6 million children 14 and under were treated in hospital emergency rooms for unintentional injuries.[9] When children visit the hospital due to accidents or illness, many are scared and need something to take their minds off their pain.

Provide comfort by making an emergency room visit a little less frightening. Create a decorated box of small gifts for the doctors and nurses to give to the children. Here are some gift suggestions:

- Miniature toy horses
- Small purses filled with goodies
- Crayons and a pad of paper or coloring book
- Paper dolls
- Picture books, including a children's Bible
- Stickers or sticker books
- Small toy tractors, cars, or airplanes
- Action figures and dolls
- Necklaces, bracelets, or a watch
- Stuffed animals for the child to snuggle

Up for Discussion

What types of gifts did your family include in their box to take to the emergency room? How did you decorate the box? What other items can you think of that might provide comfort?

Have you ever been in the emergency room? How did that make you feel? What prayer might you say for children who are taken to the hospital?

Read in John 5 about the man Jesus cured at the pool. The

man had been an invalid for 38 years and wanted to be healed at a pool in Jerusalem. "Then Jesus said to him, 'Get up! Pick up your mat and walk.' At once the man was cured; he picked up his mat and walked" (vv. 8-9). How might those around the invalid have provided comfort for him prior to the moment that Jesus healed him?

> Jesus said, "Let the little children come to me, and do not hinder them, for the kingdom of heaven belongs to such as these."
> —Matt. 19:14

24. File Adoption Papers

Many people are lonely and have no one. To fix this, your family can adopt—"take by choice into a relationship"— someone who otherwise has no family.[10] An adoptive arrangement like this provides a listening ear and comfort to those who typically have no one to talk to or spend time with. Examples:

- Adopt a grandparent. In their book *The Grandparent Factor*, Phil Waldrep and Pat Springle detail the importance of a grandparent in a child's life. Encourage your children to adopt a grandparent. This is a great family project, especially if your children don't have living biological grandparents or if their grandparents don't live close by. According to Waldrep, children also do well when a close, unrelated, older grandparent-type person has "adopted" *them*.
- Adopt a close friend. This idea isn't restricted to an adopted grandparent. Our children have adopted a close friend of the family as their "aunt," because her own family isn't supportive and doesn't spend time with her. They have also adopted as their aunt and uncle close friends of ours who live in another town and who are an extra-special addition to their lives.
- Adopt a schoolmate. Many children go home to an empty house every day after school. Make your home a safe and pleasant environment for children like these to spend their afternoons completing homework or playing with your own children.

Remember to send special-occasion cards and photos, and invite your adopted family to your children's sporting and music events. Your family may choose to copy the adoption

certificate found in the templates section for
your special adoptee(s).

Up for Discussion

Who did your family choose to adopt?
How did you make sure they truly felt adopted into your family? How did your fam-
ily's decision to adopt someone fill a void in their life? In your
family's life?

Such adoptions remind us of the pleasure of being adopted
into God's kingdom when we accept Christ as our Savior. Explain what adoption means to you and why it's important.

> *He predestined us to be adopted as his sons through Jesus Christ,*
> *in accordance with his pleasure and will.*
> —Eph. 1:5

25. Assist with Vehicle Maintenance

Vehicles have greatly changed since the early days of the automobile. But what hasn't changed is their need for periodic maintenance.

A good way for your family to offer a helping hand is to assist someone with vehicle maintenance. Is your husband a weekend mechanic? Would your children enjoy learning how to maintain a car? Perhaps a single mother, elderly person, or widow could use a tune-up on her car. Maybe someone who is struggling to afford the necessities, let alone the maintenance on his or her vehicle, could use your help. Below are some suggestions:

- Check the oil and change it if needed.
- Check the air filter, fuel filters, windshield-wiper fluid, antifreeze, hoses, and belts.
- Inflate the tires to their proper pressure.
- Check the brakes.
- Clean the interior.
- Wash the car.
- If your budget allows it, fill up the gas tank.

Up for Discussion

What did you learn from this activity? How might you and your family incorporate this into a monthly or yearly event?

Read the story of Jesus' arrival on a donkey in John 12:12-19. In those days animals were a critical mode of transportation. How would life have been difficult if the animals were not fed, watered, and kept in good condition? How does this correlate to today's mode of transportation? How would someone who depends on a vehicle be severely inconvenienced if the car was not in working order?

Blessed is he who comes in the name of the Lord!
—John 12:13

26. Remember Your Sisters and Brothers in Christ

What a blessing it is when the Lord provides us with fellow believers in Christ! To honor them, spend some time doing something special for those fellow believers. Think about those who worship with you regularly. What can you do for your Sunday School class? How can your children do something for their brothers and sisters in Christ?

At our women's Bible study we recently created homemade magnets with caricatures of the women in our small group. Our daughters drew headshots of us, which we cut into rectangles and placed in magnetic photo holders. (See the templates section for an example of this activity.) Enlist your family's various artistic skills to create caricatures for Sunday School, Bible study, Christian scouting group, or other friends.

Another idea for this activity is to take a photo of your group, make copies, frame them, and present one to each member.

Up for Discussion

Why is it important to have Christian fellowship? What are some ways you see the evidence of Christian fellowship in your family? Why is prayer a necessary part of fellowship? What other ideas can you think of for this activity?

The Bible talks about the necessity of Christian fellowship. Read 1 John 1:7, and discuss how this relates to our lives.

2 Corinthians 6:14 states, "Do not be yoked together with unbelievers. For what do righteousness and wickedness have in common? Or what fellowship can light have with darkness?" Think about the importance of spending time with fellow Christians rather than those who are not Christians. Why

might Paul have stressed this importance in this verse?

If we walk in the light, as he is in the light, we have fellowship with one another, and the blood of Jesus, his Son, purifies us from all sin.
—1 John 1:7

27. Offer to Assist with Clutter Control

Often in these times of busyness the last thing on one's mind is clutter control. Though it's an undesirable task, it's necessary, and your family can brighten someone's day by helping him or her control clutter.

Make it a family event. Offer to help someone clean out his or her garage. Perhaps your family could aid someone in controlling and eliminating the clutter in his or her home office or living room. Following are some suggestions for each member of your family. Nominate a member for each of the following:

- Help file paperwork.
- Help with dusting, vacuuming, and other cleanup duties.
- Carry boxes and bags to the garbage can. Or carry them to the car for delivery to a worthy cause.
- Be the "clutter patrol." Along with the person you are helping, decide which items are no longer needed.

Because eliminating items can be such a mundane task, assisting someone in creating a clutter-free home can ensure that the task is finished with efficiency.

Up for Discussion

Who did your family decide to help? Why? Which part of their home did you clean up? What did you learn from this activity? Why can it be overwhelming at times to filter out unwanted items? How might helping someone else with their clutter help your family with theirs?

Read Prov. 23:4-5. Why do you think we are warned

against becoming rich? How can collecting things create a problem for us? Why is a focus on material items dangerous? Where should our focus be? Think about the only true thing that ultimately matters—the gift of eternal life.

> Do not wear yourself out to get rich; have the wisdom to show restraint.
> Cast but a glance at riches, and they are gone, for they will surely
> sprout wings and fly off to the sky like an eagle.
> —Prov. 23:4-5

28. Support a Worthy Cause

Last year through Operation Christmas Child more than 7.6 million shoe box gifts were collected worldwide to help share the love of Jesus Christ and the joy of Christmas with children.[11] What an amazing project this is! But efforts to help the underprivileged—much like this one—don't go without their own needs.

Encourage your family to support a worthy cause. They can join together to serve a cause, such as Operation Christmas Child, sponsored by Samaritan's Purse. Or make it a neighborhood event. Encourage your children to write letters to family, friends, and the people in your neighborhood asking for their involvement.

Our family undertook this project last winter. Our oldest daughter wrote the letters and attached Samaritan's Purse brochures, while our youngest daughter illustrated them. We made numerous copies of these handwritten letters and then walked through the neighborhood delivering each letter accompanied with a plate of goodies we had baked.

In your letters you may want to include the following:

- The suggested contents of the boxes. You can find suggestions for what to include on the Samaritan's Purse web site and also in their brochure.
- Delivery sites. The boxes can be delivered to a local participating church, a drop-off point, or your home. If you use your home for a delivery site—an ideal location for first-time donors—be sure to include your address, drop-off times, and the assurance that you will deliver their box for them.

- Donor labels and forms. The Samaritan's Purse web site provides downloadable copies of both the box label and the donor form. (The donor form asks for the donor's name, address, and the age of the child for whom the box is intended.) Download these forms and make photocopies to include in your letter.
- Your children's favorite Bible verse(s).
- Information to encourage the donor to include a letter to the box recipient.

Be sure to have extra shoe boxes on hand for those who need them. Local retailers are a good source for extra boxes —they were more than happy to donate boxes to us for this project. A word of caution: be sure to collect boxes several months before you begin this project.

When we undertook this project, several of the folks in our neighborhood wanted to help but were unable to go shopping for the items for the shoe boxes. This turned out to be an adventure for our family. The neighbors gave us money, and our daughters picked out items for their boxes.

There are many other great causes for which your family can collect. Whatever worthy cause you choose to support, include your entire family, and make a difference in the lives of others.

Up for Discussion

What was the most challenging part of completing this activity? If you opted to do the Samaritan's Purse project, discuss the difference that a small shoe box full of gifts can make for a child who doesn't have much. How does this provide an opportunity for sharing the gospel? What other type of collection could your family choose to partake in?

How is delivering letters and goodies and asking neighbors and friends to help (even unbelievers) an excellent way to introduce the love of Christ?

Read Ps. 41:1. Why do you think it's important to have "regard for the weak"? Ponder for a moment what the world would be like if we never cared for anyone who was weaker or less "able" than ourselves. What would happen to those in that position? Why should we strive to never forget the ones God has called us to help?

> Blessed is he who has regard for the weak;
> the LORD delivers him in times of trouble.
>
> —Ps. 41:1

29. Listen

"Examples of noise levels considered dangerous by experts are a lawn mower, a rock concert, firearms, firecrackers, headset listening systems, motorcycles, tractors, household appliances (garbage disposals, blenders, food processors/choppers, etc.) and noisy toys. All can deliver sound over 90 decibels and some up to 140 decibels."[12]

Though these are examples of the noisier aspects of life, they are still examples of things we all hear on a regular basis. Yet there are many ears that don't hear these things and many more that don't hear the voices of those who need someone to listen.

Listen—such a simple yet important concept.

A wise person once said there is a reason God gave us one mouth and two ears—to listen more than we speak. Give someone the gift of listening. This is something everyone in your family can commit to doing. Do you know someone who has been having a difficult time and needs an attentive ear? Do you know a child who just needs someone to listen? Do you know an elderly person who lives alone and would love someone to listen, someone with whom to share his or her thoughts? So often we don't *really* take the time to listen to what someone has to say.

Have your family take a vow—a vow to listen. It's something that can be done any time of the year. Exercise that vow by taking some time to listen to someone who just needs to talk.

Who did you make a vow to listen to this past week? Why is it important to listen—and not just *hear*—what someone is saying? Read James 1:19. Why should you make it a habit to be slow to speak but quick to listen?

Luke 10:21 states, "'I praise you, Father, Lord of heaven and earth, because you have hidden these things from the wise and learned, and revealed them to little children.'" Why is listening to what the Lord says through His Word important? Why is reading the Bible to understand it and absorb it better than reading it just to read it? How can you better listen for God's voice in everyday life?

> *Everyone should be quick to listen, slow to speak.*
> —James 1:19

30. Help with Heating Bills

Many of us take for granted being able to flip a switch and feel warm air flow from a heater. We don't think twice about the warmth that comes from a fireplace or a coal-burning stove. However, not everyone has this luxury.

Winter can be an especially difficult time for some people. The cost of heating a home can at times be something that is forced to fall by the wayside when there is not enough income.

Make a difference this winter by helping someone pay his or her heating bill. Some utility companies offer a fund for customers to donate to which assists those who have trouble paying their bill. You may also wish to pay the bill of someone specific.

Up for Discussion

Who did your family choose to assist in this activity? How could the generosity of your family be an answer to someone's prayers?

Read 1 Kings 17:7-16, the story of how the generosity of a widow toward Elijah produced benefits for her and her son. The only food she had left was a small amount of flour and oil—barely enough to feed her family. However, she graciously baked a loaf of bread for Elijah before feeding herself and her son. Discuss the outcome of this story and how the woman's faith that God would provide enabled her to be charitable to someone she didn't even know. Think about how the little amount of food this woman had would be detrimental to her survival, just as inadequate fuel during a long, cold winter would be detrimental to someone's survival today.

Now read 1 Tim. 6:17. Why should those who are rich not be arrogant? Why should hope be only in the Lord, and not in things, such as wealth? How could you explain to someone who doesn't know the Lord why hope in eternal life is much more valuable than hope in material items?

Command those who are rich in this present world not to be arrogant nor to put their hope in wealth, which is so uncertain, but to put their hope in God, who richly provides us with everything for our enjoyment.
—1 Tim. 6:17

31. Found a Lending Library

A peek into your entertainment center or a glance at your bookshelf might
reveal an idea that could make a difference.
Your family may have an abundance of movies and books, but
other families aren't as fortunate as to be able to enjoy movies or books of their own. And some families just simply need
something new to watch!

Provide others with some enjoyment by lending movies and
books to family, friends, and neighbors. Create a lending library,
offering family-oriented choices to borrowers rather than movies that are thick with violence and language. Be on the lookout
for movies and books that can encourage, inspire, and promote
family togetherness. Not only will you be connecting with others in a positive way, but this also gives your family a chance to
witness through two different types of media.

Video/DVD suggestions:
- *Facing the Giants*
- *The Nativity Story*
- *Duma*
- *Wild Hearts Can't Be Broken*
- *Love Comes Softly*
- *One Night with the King*
- *Though None Go with Me*
- *Little Women*

Adult book suggestions:
- *Where to Find It in the Bible,* by Ken Anderson
- *What the Bible Is All About,* by Henrietta C. Mears
- *Making Disciples—One Conversation at a Time,* by D. Michael
  Henderson

- *When People Are Big and God Is Small*, by Edward T. Welch
- *Shepherding a Child's Heart*, by Tedd Tripp
- *The Complete Husband*, by Lou Priolo
- *Evolution Exposed*, by Roger Patterson
- *Spiritual Growth of Children*, by John Trent, Rick Osborne, Kurt Bruner

Children's picture book suggestions:
- *The Princess and the Kiss* by Jennie Bishop
- *The Squire and the Scroll*, by Jennie Bishop
- *The Farmer*, by Mark Ludy
- *The Lost Sheep and Other Stories Jesus Told*, by Phil A. Smouse
- *A Faith to Grow On*, by John MacArthur
- *Sticky Situations: 365 Devotions for Kids and Families*, by Betsy Schmitt
- *A Little Girl After God's Own Heart*, by Elizabeth George

Up for Discussion

What makes your family library different from a public library? How might others grow in their faith through your library? Why is it important to share wholesome items with others? What example can your family set by creating a neighborhood lending library?

Read Phil. 4:8. Why is it important to protect our eyes and ears from things that are not pleasing to God? How can your family library provide a positive option for others in today's media?

Whatever is true, whatever is noble, whatever is right, whatever is pure,
whatever is lovely, whatever is admirable—
if anything is excellent or praiseworthy—think about such things.
—Phil. 4:8

32. Visit a Homeless Shelter

Across the country thousands of people live homeless. While homelessness offers very little comforts, many homeless individuals receive food and a bed at a shelter. However, those shelters are often short-handed and could always use an additional helping hand, if not a family of helping hands.

Until our family had made a visit to our local homeless shelter, we didn't realize just what a vital part of the community it is. The capacity of the shelter is 35, and at any given time most of the beds are occupied.

Spend some time taking your family to the local homeless shelter or soup kitchen. The visit will provide many good ideas for ways to minister to those going through tough times. One way is to donate food. When I was shown the food pantry in our shelter, I was amazed at the amount of food. But the amount of food in the pantry didn't matter—considering the number of people who eat the meals each day, it wouldn't be long before the canned goods that neatly lined the shelves were depleted.

Next time you go shopping, ask your children to pick out one or two items that could be donated to the shelter. Stock up on those items. Several times we've noticed tremendous sales on certain food items in grocery-store ads. During those sales we purchase food for ourselves and also for the shelter. Check with the director at the shelter for food ideas, or consider the following:

- Canned soups
- Canned meals, such as SpaghettiO's or Ravioli

- Cereal (both cold and hot varieties)
- Boxed foods, such as macaroni and cheese or noodles
- Milk
- Eggs
- Potatoes
- Bread

Another way to minister is to serve dinner at the shelter or soup kitchen. When our family served a meal there, it was an eye-opening experience for us. The residents were gracious. Never did we meet a more thankful group of people, all for the simple task of serving them a hot meal. We were also given the opportunity to leave tracts and Christian books in the community hallway. This experience brought to mind how Jesus continually fed the poor and how today He continues to feed our souls with His Word.

Up for Discussion

When you visited the shelter for the first time, was it what you expected it to be? Why or why not? What important things did you learn from serving or donating food to the homeless shelter? What other food items could your family donate in the future? How might your family encourage others to support their local homeless shelter?

Read John 6 about the 5,000 people Jesus fed with five loaves of bread and two fish. Discuss how, when your family fed those at the shelter, your work reflected what Jesus did when He fed the multitude and how we should strive to be like Him.

I was hungry and you gave me something to eat, I was thirsty and you gave me something to drink, I was a stranger and you invited me in.
—Matt. 25:35

33. Send Flowers

According to Guinness World Records, "The tallest self-supported rose bush measured 4.03 meters (13 feet, 3 inches) on December 5, 2005, and grows in the garden of Paul and Sharon Palumbo . . . in San Diego, California."[13]

Like this impressive bush, flowers hold meaning and make an impact on someone's life.

Many people recovering in hospital rooms have no one thinking of them or no relatives nearby. Fix this by sending an anonymous bouquet of flowers to them. Deliver or send carnations, roses, or seasonal flowers, along with a helium balloon or two, to the hospital room. A potted plant also works well. Include a note telling the recipient that you're thinking about and praying for him or her. Ask the receptionist at the front desk to deliver the flowers or plant to someone who hasn't received any.

Up for Discussion

What note did you include for this project? Would this be a worthwhile project to do on a quarterly basis? Which do you think is better—a potted plant or a bouquet? Why? Why would having to make sure a potted plant lives take an ill person's mind off the pain he or she is experiencing?

How can an anonymously given plant brighten someone's day, especially someone who is ill? How can a living plant testify to God's goodness?

Read Isa. 41:10. How can this verse comfort someone facing a troublesome circumstance? What other verses throughout the Bible promise of God's unending love?

Do not fear, for I am with you; do not be dismayed, for I am your God. I will strengthen you and help you; I will uphold you with my righteous right hand.
—Isa. 41:10

34. Give a Bible

Hundreds of thousands of Bibles are sold or given away each day—and that's just in the United States! Bibles have a strong impact on individuals, as their selling numbers testify. A good way for your family to minister is by adding to this number and giving away a Bible or two.

Place a Bible in every Christmas gift you deliver this Christmas. You can find some excellent deals on Bibles purchased in bulk through a variety of Christian bookstores, such as <cbd.com>. What a great witnessing tool!

Up for Discussion

What was the response you received to this activity? What could you tell someone who was less than happy to receive a Bible with his or her gift?

What other places could you distribute Bibles? Take a moment to think about the Bibles that are placed by The Gideons International in hotel rooms, doctor's offices, and hospital rooms. Do you think those Bibles have had any impact on the guests and patients? Why or why not? How could a Bible placed in these locations provide comfort to the people who find them? How could a Bible change their lives?

Read Phil. 2:4. Why do you think it's important to consider the needs and interests of others rather than just those of our own?

> Each of you should look not only to your own interests,
> but also to the interests of others.
> —Phil. 2:4

35. Pound the Pavement

Walking is healthful! It helps manage blood pressure, diabetes, weight, and stress and helps you stay strong and active.[14] Involve the whole family, and invite a lonely or elderly neighbor on a walk. Not only is walking a fantastic way to exercise, but it also allows time to encourage conversation with someone you don't know. Get to know that person who lives next door or the one who rarely has visitors. Brighten his or her spirit, and enjoy the beautiful scenery God created at the same time.

Do you have small children in your family? Push them in the stroller as your family walks with your neighbor. Dad doesn't particularly enjoy walking? Invite him to ride his bike alongside. Does your teen have a more active idea in mind? Suggest that he rollerblade while the rest of the family walks. The point is to do this project as a family and to extend the invitation to someone else to join.

Up for Discussion

How did this activity provide family unity? How could you make it a weekly event? What impact would it have on the lonely or elderly person you asked to join your family?

Discuss 1 Cor. 6:19-20. Why does the Bible place an emphasis on keeping your temple healthy? What does it mean "you were bought at a price"? What are some other ways, besides exercise, that you can keep your temple healthy? Discuss these ways, including spiritually, mentally, and physically. How does this activity help others keep healthy the bodies God gave them?

Do you not know that your body is a temple of the Holy Spirit, who is in you, whom you have received from God? You are not your own; you were bought at a price. Therefore honor God with your body.
—1 Cor. 6:19-20

36. Become a Fundraiser Organizer

Investigate worthy causes in or around your town. Find out how you can help. For instance, is there an organization that

- Accepts gently used business clothes for needy women who are entering the workforce after being in jail?
- Collects aluminum cans to raise money?
- Seeks Christian books to be distributed in jails?
- Needs food for their dwindling food pantry?

Check with organizations that may have needs, such as for the above items. Arrange for your family to set up a collection point and deliver the items at a specified time.

Are any of the following possible locations available as a collection point? Be sure to check with the pastor or director of the organization first.

- Your Sunday School class
- Your church foyer or other area church foyers
- Location where your prayer group meets
- Your children's school or public library
- A local restaurant
- A community center
- Area businesses
- City hall or the courthouse

If the collection point is available, look into advertising the information through the church bulletin or the organization's newsletter. The bottom line: Bring awareness to the need.

What fundraiser did your family choose to help for this activity? Was it successful? Were churches, businesses, or organizations available as collection points? How did you advertise the fundraiser? How does providing a collection point take the burden off those that wanted to help but could not deliver the items themselves? How does banding together with others to benefit a need in the community draw people to Christ?

Read Mark 12:41-44 about the poor widow's donation. Why do you think this story was significant enough to be included in the Bible? Why did the widow in effect give much more than the wealthy people?

> Jesus said, "I tell you the truth, this poor widow has put more into the treasury than all the others. They all gave out of their wealth; but she, out of her poverty, put in everything—all she had to live on."
>
> —Mark 12:43-44

37. Take Part in Ministry Outreach

A simple way for your family to spread the gospel and make a difference is through tracts, Christian books, or Christian magazines. Although books and magazines will work for the following suggestions, tracts work best because they are small and direct with their meaning. Leave information at various public facilities, such as

- Laundromats
- Hotels, motels, cabins, and bed and breakfasts
- Doctor's offices
- Homeless shelters
- Restaurants
- Airports
- Counters in public restrooms
- Concerts

Using this activity, your family is able to minister to others in a gentle way. Consider the following story:

Recently an AiG [Answers in Genesis] staff member used a simple brochure in a non-threatening way to reach someone he had never met for Christ. When a maid was cleaning the hotel room in which the staff member was staying, she discovered a tip tucked into an AiG brochure. As she read, she became more interested and decided to visit the AiG web site. There, this young woman with no church background said all the questions that had caused her to doubt Christianity were answered.

With some remaining questions about salvation, she decided to meet the staff member face-to-face. There he shared the gospel, and she accepted the Lord into her life.

The following Wednesday she took her parents to a nearby church, and they, too, gave their hearts to Jesus![15]

Not sure where to purchase tracts? There are many outlets, including <wayofthemaster.com>. Remind your family that a tract an individual finds may be the only glimpse of God they ever see.

Another way to spread the gospel is to order magazine subscriptions. This gift can be for an acquaintance, friend, or family member. Ever wondered how to introduce God to someone who lives far away? Subscribe to a Christian magazine for him or her. There are several to choose from, and magazines are an informal yet important way to bring God to someone's life on a regular basis. Some subscription companies offer special deals if you order more than one subscription or if you order a gift subscription. You may never know how many lives are changed through something as simple as a magazine.

Do you receive a Christian magazine? Pass it on to someone else after you are finished reading it. Encourage that person to pass it on yet again when he or she is finished with it.

Up for Discussion

What did your family do for this activity? How can tracts help others come to know Christ? What about magazine subscriptions or books?

Consider designing your own tracts. What verses would you include? What inspirational words would you write? What creative ideas could you invent to entice someone to take a second glance at a tract? What other strategic places could you leave the tract so that it's noticed?

A common tract that's often used is a fake dollar bill with the words about the gospel written on the backside. How would this type of tract inspire someone to pick it up and investigate it?

Read 1 Cor. 1:17. Why do you think this verse says "not with words of human wisdom"? How does our wisdom compare to the wisdom of God? Why do you think this verse states "lest the cross of Christ be emptied of its power"? What does this mean to you?

How can you ensure that this activity makes an impact? How is prayer for wisdom from God an important part of the equation?

Christ did not send me to baptize, but to preach the gospel—not with words of human wisdom, lest the cross of Christ be emptied of its power.

—1 Cor. 1:17

38. Create a Movie or Game Night

One of the traditions in our home is movie night. After dinner, our family gathers around the television set with huge bowls of popcorn and settles into a movie. After the popcorn has been eaten, we all snuggle together. In the winter we fetch our blankets from their nook inside the entertainment center and settle in to this time that everyone looks forward to and enjoys.

Use this idea as inspiration to create a movie night for a family you know. Include the following:

- A box of microwave popcorn
- A large-sized candy bar for each member of the family
- A two-liter bottle of soda (two of them for larger families)
- A good DVD or video (see activity 31 for movie suggestions)
- Movie tickets, such as the example found in the templates section

Can't find a good movie? Purchase a board or card game for a family. We also enjoy playing games such as Uno, Memory, and Sorry. If you choose to use a game instead of a movie, include a two-liter bottle of soda and some nacho chips with cheese dip.

Take this activity further by making a game instead. If you want to ensure that the activity includes your whole family, or if you don't have it in your budget to purchase a game, enlist the artists in your family to make the game. Our family made our own Memory game, complete with two-of-a-kind drawings of each picture. We drew pictures of animals, shapes, scenery, people, and

cars. You can also write Bible verses on the
cards for a Bible memory game. Use cardstock paper and colored pencils to create the
game. There won't be another game *exactly*
like it anywhere—guaranteed!

Whichever activity you choose—mov-
ie night or game night—have fun creating a night the entire
family can enjoy.

Up for Discussion

Did your family decide on the movie or the game night?
What was the reaction of your recipients? How did completing the above activity promote togetherness in both your family and the family who received your gift?

Read Exod. 1—2. Just prior to Moses's birth, the Pharaoh
ordered, "Every boy that is born you must throw into the Nile,
but let every girl live" (Exod. 1:22). In the following chapter,
in an effort to save her son's life, Moses's mother hides him in
a basket. Moses's sister, Miriam, stands guard over her younger
brother and watches as the Pharaoh's daughter discovers the
baby while walking to the Nile. Explain what happens next: If
Miriam hadn't been keeping watch over Moses, what do you
think would have happened? If Moses's mother hadn't placed
him in a basket, but had kept him instead, what do you think
would have happened to him? God's plan for Moses included using Moses's mother and sister to help carry it out. Think
about the significance of family according to God's Word. Why
should a family, if possible, band together in both the good
and bad moments? How does this correlate with this activity?

"I will be a Father to you, and you will be my sons and daughters,"
says the Lord Almighty.
—2 Cor. 6:18

39. Pray Without Ceasing

Much has been said about the importance of prayer and the difference it makes in the lives of others. Gather your family together for the following prayer activities:

- Have each family member pick a person at random and pray for him or her all week. This person can be a family member, friend, teacher, coworker, or a person from church. Or pray for someone who isn't as directly related to you—someone you heard through the media or by word-of-mouth has just been in a car accident or has been ill. You don't have to know the person to pray for him or her. God knows who the person is and his or her immediate needs.

- Encourage your family to take a moment to pray anytime you hear the sound of an ambulance siren. This has become a habit in our family, as is praying for the helicopter pilots who fly patients to larger hospitals. Our prayers sound something like this: *Father, we ask for your healing hand upon whoever is being transported at this time. We also pray that you would guide the paramedics and work through the doctors' hands so the patient may be healed according to your will. We also pray, Lord, that if the patient doesn't know you, he or she will come to know you. In Jesus' name we pray. Amen.*

- Schedule a prayer vigil.

- Start a prayer chain. Prepare a list of names and phone numbers of relatives and friends who are willing to be part of a prayer chain. Notify the people on the list, and ask them to pray when there is a prayer concern. Also ask them to call or e-mail the next person on the list. Does your child have a friend who is struggling in school? Does your friend have a son who recently broke his arm at football practice? Is someone's grandparent facing a health crisis? Are there travelers or unbelievers or soldiers in your midst? All these people will greatly benefit from prayer, as can anyone who is struggling spiritually, physically, mentally, or emotionally.

- Keep a family prayer journal. This is simple to make and fun to use. Decorate a notebook cover with photos or caricatures of your family. Purchase letter stickers for the cover, spelling out the words "Prayer Journal for the [your last name] Family" and the words of 1 Thess. 5:17. (See the templates section for an example of a family prayer journal cover.) Be sure to keep several pages in the back of your journal for a section titled "Answered Prayers." Once God has answered a prayer request, list that request in this section. Watch in amazement as God answers prayer in His time and according to His will. Be sure to praise Him for the wonderful way He hears and responds to prayer.

Up for Discussion

Discuss the importance of prayer. Who did your family pray for during this past week? How can you be sure your prayers made a difference? Why is it important to praise God for the prayers He has answered?

After a month or so has passed, look back at your prayer journal under the "Answered Prayers" section. Which answered prayer was the most surprising? Remember: God doesn't always answer prayers in the way we would assume. Which prayer was answered most quickly? How can you praise God for the answered prayers? Locate the areas in the

Bible where Jesus prayed. How does the fact that He prayed encourage your own faith in prayer?

Read 1 Thess. 5:16-18. Why should we be thankful, even during the difficult times we experience?

> Be joyful always; pray continually; give thanks in all circumstances,
> for this is God's will for you in Christ Jesus.
> —1 Thess. 5:16-18

40. Help a Single Mom

In the United States there are 10 million single mothers with children aged 18 and under living with them. This figure is up from 3 million in 1970.[16] This is a large number of single mothers—who should not go unnoticed. Being a single mom presents multiple challenges, and encouragement is always welcome.

Encourage your family to do something nice for a single mom. One idea is to simply present her with a gift, such as a women's devotional book. Here are some great suggestions:

- *The Busy Mom's Devotional: Ten Minutes a Week to a Life of Devotion*, by Lisa T. Bergren
- *Single Moms Raising Sons: Preparing Boys to Be Men When There's No Man Around*, by Dana S. Chisholm
- *Quiet Moments for a Busy Mom's Soul*, by Emilie Barnes
- *Mom to Mom: Committing Our Children to God*, by Cheryl Gochnauer
- *Hugs for Single Moms*, by Melanie Hemry

Another way to help out is to deliver a box of food at the mother's workplace. When deciding what to include, think of items that will be helpful for her children's lunches or snack times. Some ideas:

- Cereal
- Fruit snacks
- Granola bars
- Fruit cups
- Graham crackers

Many single moms are unable to attend their children's extracurricular activities. Offer to film or photograph that basketball game or band performance. The difference it will make to her will be huge.

Up for Discussion

What did your family choose to do to help a single mom? Are you from a single-parent family? If so, what insight do you have that could be helpful in assisting children and their parents in other single-parent homes? Are you close friends with someone who is in a single-parent home? What other nice things could your family do for the family? How could you apply this activity to a family with a single dad?

Deut. 10:18 states, "He defends the cause of the fatherless and the widow, and loves the alien, giving him food and clothing." Discuss how this verse is applicable to this activity.

Read 1 John 4:11-12. How is God's love in us if we love one another? Who would benefit from seeing that God lives in us?

> Dear friends, since God so loved us, we also ought to love one another.
> No one has ever seen God; but if we love one another,
> God lives in us and his love is made complete in us.
> —1 John 4:11-12

41. Celebrate the Christmas Season

Do you have writers, actors, singers, narrators, seamstresses, directors, or prop builders lurking around your home? Volunteer your family's time to help put on a Christmas program for members of your church. Speak with your pastor about posting a sign-up sheet on a bulletin board in the church foyer. On the sheet, request that people of all ages join in for this fun presentation. (See the templates section for an example of a sign-up sheet for this activity.) Use this sign-up sheet to gather your participants for the production.

A Christmas program is guaranteed to bring a smile to the faces of the congregation. Some things to think about when organizing your program:

- What is a good time to schedule the performance? Will there be only one?
- How many practices will you have? When will they be held? Remember to begin rehearsing early—beginning in October will give your crew plenty of time to perfect their performance.
- Will you be presenting a musical or a dramatization of the Christmas story or both?
- Who will write the script?
- Will one or more narrators be a necessary part of the performance?
- Does a member of your family know how to use the sound equipment? If not, can someone in the church volunteer?
- Will the church choir be available for back-up singing if necessary?

- Can a member of your family sew costumes? If not, enlist the assistance of someone who can.
- Will props be necessary? Does the church have some in storage that may be used, or will some need to be made?
- Will refreshments, such as Christmas cookies, apple cider, or hot chocolate, be served after the program? Who will bake them?
- Can you announce the program to the community? Outreach is a vital part of ministering to those who don't believe. Remember to announce it at least a month in advance.
- Is there someone who will be available to film the performance for those who are unable to attend?
- Who will be part of the clean-up crew after the program?

Remember that the main focus is on the reason we celebrate Christmas: the wonderful blessing of God's Son sent to us as a baby. Keep the focus on this important point, and the program will be a success!

Up for Discussion

What type of program did you provide for your church? Who wrote it and why? Was your program well received? How can you make it a yearly event? Why is inviting those who don't go to your church important? How did you publicize the event?

1 Corinthians 14:12 states, "Try to excel in gifts that build up the church." How does this activity promote the use of the gifts God has given us?

Read the entire Christmas story in your Bible, beginning with Luke 1. Imagine for a moment that you lived during the time of Jesus' birth. How do you think you would have responded to the news? Fast forward to today's time—do people respond better now than they did at that time?

She will give birth to a son,
and you are to give him the name Jesus,
because he will save his people from their sins.
—Matt. 1:21

42. Beautify Our Surroundings

Has your family ever driven along the freeway and noticed the abundant amount of litter lining the road? Or have you walked through the park only to be shocked at the food wrappers and other trash that fills the spaces between grass and trees? Realize the importance of keeping God's world beautiful, and schedule a litter clean-up day for your family. Below are some suggestions for the day.

- Dress appropriately for the weather. Layer warm clothes for cold weather, and wear hats and sun protection in warm weather. Remember good shoes no matter what the season is. Long pants are necessary, especially in weedy areas where ticks, snakes, and poison ivy may lurk.
- Wear gloves.
- Instruct your children to clean up only paper items. Sadly, there are many other non-paper items that could harm those in your family. Do not try to clean up these things.
- Be sure an adult is with your children at all times.
- Bring plenty of garbage bags.
- Wash your hands thoroughly after you have completed the litter clean-up and again before eating.

It makes a huge difference to everyone to see a cleaner earth that God made. Encourage your family to be part of this project!

Up for Discussion

Why is it important to keep God's earth clean? Where did you family decide to do this activity? A park? A playground? A walking-path area? Downtown? What else can you do to beautify our world for future generations? How does recycling play a role?

Think back to another time, such as 75 or 150 years ago. How was the litter problem different at that time than it is today?

Read Gen. 2:15. Why do you think God wants us to be good stewards of the amazing world He created?

> The LORD God took the man and put him in the
> Garden of Eden to work it and take care of it.
> —Gen. 2:15

43. Smile

Looking for an inexpensive way to make someone's day? Try a smile. The world needs more smiles. If you see someone on the street, smile. Smile at those in the grocery store. Smile when you're driving down the road. It really does make the world a better place. In this hectic world we live in, it's nice to see a smile, and you'll be amazed at how many of your smiles are returned.

Up for Discussion

Think about how this activity would have dramatically changed if you had chosen to frown at everyone instead.

Read John 9 about Jesus' healing of the blind man. Imagine for a moment the reaction Jesus must have received after healing this man and so many others throughout the New Testament. He probably smiled at the ones He healed, knowing that the miracles He performed made such an impact in the lives of those who needed Him most. Considering this, discuss how just a mere smile can change the direction of a person's day.

Read Eccles. 3:12. Why do you think it's important to "do good" during our short time on this earth? Imagine for a moment a world in which no one cared for anyone else, a world in which no one ever did nice things for others. Would you want to live in that kind of world?

> I know that there is nothing better for men than to be happy
> and do good while they live.
> —Eccles. 3:12

44. Donate Your Time

One of the ways in which God asks us to serve is with our time. Is there a ministry in your community that could use some of your family's time? For example, the ministry known as "Vision Beyond Borders" seeks "to serve the worldwide church by providing the necessary tools and training for the local people to fulfill Christ's 'Great Commission' in their own countries."[17] One of the ways volunteers can assist Vision Beyond Borders is to donate their time packing seeds and clothing that will be delivered to countries overseas. Something as easy as packing seed packets into sandwich bags can be accomplished with even a child's help. Another task is cutting out flannelgraphs, which are used to communicate God's Word to those in other countries.

Locate a local ministry that's in need of your time. There are many just like Vision Beyond Borders who await a small donation of your family's time. Ask your pastor for suggestions of organizations, or research some on the Internet. Encourage your family to donate some time to an organization, and watch as a difference is made!

Up for Discussion

What organization did your family choose to help? Why? How often is your family planning to serve for this ministry?

How do you think packing seeds in sandwich bags for those overseas can assist those in other countries? What might flannelgraphs be used for, and how can these activities spread the gospel?

Why is time just as important a donation or an even more important donation than money?

Read Rom. 10:15. How are feet "beautiful" when they're used to share the gospel? Why and how should we be Jesus' feet in sharing the Good News?

> *How beautiful are the feet of those who bring the good news!*
> —Rom. 10:15

45. Bake Treats

Do you like gingerbread cookies? Do you know where they came from? "The Crusaders are credited with bringing gingerbread to Europe, although not in the form we enjoy today. At one time it was made with breadcrumbs and sweetened with honey."[18] Though this little-known fact doesn't alter the yummy taste of the cookies, it's something to think about the next time you eat one.

Something else to think about as you eat a cookie is how much you love them. And an easy way for your family to spread Christmas cheer is to spread your love of cookies. Gather your family, and bake homemade goodies to deliver to your neighbors. Here are some examples:

- Sugar cookies
- Gingerbread cookies
- Fudge
- Chocolate-covered pretzels
- Homemade candies

Purchase festive plates, and place several treats on each. Cover the plates with cellophane, and add bows and ribbons. Another fun addition our family does each year is design and cut out homemade Christmas tags that we attach to each plate. Last year's design was the manger scene that our daughters drew, and it included a Bible verse relating to Christ's birth. Each tag also said, "Merry Christmas from the Zeller Family."

When you have finished wrapping the treats, set out, as a family, to deliver the plates with a cheery holiday greeting. What a nice way to spread Christmas cheer and become reacquainted with your neighbors at the same time!

What was your favorite part of this activity? Why? How else might you decorate and personalize the gift tags? How would this activity help your family become acquainted or reacquainted with neighbors you don't see or speak to very often? How could this activity be helpful in showing Christ's love to a difficult neighbor?

Read the parable of the great banquet in Luke 14:15-23. Discuss the decision of the men who were initially invited to the banquet. How did their decision benefit others who would not have otherwise experienced anything so grand?

> Go out quickly into the streets and alleys of the town and bring in the poor,
> the crippled, the blind and the lame.
> —Luke 14:21

46. Host a Garage Sale

Summer brings hot weather and barbecues, swimming pools and water balloon fights. And it also brings a slew of garage sales for those selling items they no longer use. Make use of this commonality by hosting a garage sale to raise money for a need or a local charity. Below are some ideas of people or organizations you can help.

- A local Christian school scholarship fund.
- The medical expenses of someone with an illness.
- Missionaries, through your church.
- The missions trip costs for someone in your church.
- A family whose father recently lost his job or was injured.
- An elderly woman in your church who is unable to afford her prescription medicine.
- A young couple who have two children and are having difficulty paying their rent.

Ask family and friends to bring anything of value that they no longer need or want. Combine these items with those your family has donated. Be sure to make it clear that only sellable items are needed. Clothes that are stained or full of holes are not welcome; neither are broken appliances.

For a treat, have your children bake chocolate chip cookies. Allow them to sell the cookies, along with punch, to customers. Post signs stating that all money will be donated, and be sure to list the cause.

Your family could also host a *free* garage sale. Find things that you would like to give away. Everyone loves a freebie, and many people observe, "One person's trash is another person's treasure."

Up for Discussion

What was the response to your garage sale—from those who donated items and from those who purchased items? How was each family member involved in this activity? What charity did your family choose for the proceeds? What other charities could you donate to in the future? What did your family choose to do with the leftover items from the garage sale?

If your family held a *free* garage sale, discuss how receiving something for free could bring happiness to someone's day.

Read and think about Matt. 6:21. What do you think is meant by this verse? How does this fit into the role that materialism plays in our society? How can having a garage sale help one's heart release the things that don't matter?

> *Where your treasure is, there your heart will be also.*
> —Matt. 6:21

47. Plan a Spa Day

Do you know a lady who's been a little down lately? What about someone who needs a break from the hectic world around her? Offer to treat her to a spa day. This is a great mother-daughter suggestion and can be done in affordable or expensive ways.

The first step is a facial. Find out if the recipient has any allergies so you can plan accordingly. Then, using a coupon similar to the one found in the templates section, invite the recipient to your home. Provide a relaxing time for her facial, having cotton swabs and fresh-scented lotion on hand. Be sure to play calming music in the background.

The second stop is a new do. With the aid of your teenage daughter and at the preference of the recipient, use curlers or a hair-straightener to create a temporary new look.

Third, offer a manicure and pedicure, complete with two or three choices of polish color.

And last, offer some tea, hot chocolate, or coffee, and a light snack to enjoy along with you and your daughter.

If you don't have the resources to provide a spa in your home, or if other circumstances prevent this, a second idea is to purchase a relaxing experience for your intended recipient:

- A half-hour massage. To find a massage therapist in your area, search on the American Massage Therapy Association web site at <www.amtamassage.org>.
- An appointment at the beauty parlor. This is especially kind if the recipient doesn't have the funds or the time to have her hair trimmed.

- A manicure or pedicure (or both). Schedule an appointment and provide the funds for your recipient to have her nails done.
- A trip to the local café for a hot chocolate or latte.

Whichever idea you choose, encourage your children to be a part of this gift-giving idea. Sometimes all it takes to boost someone's outlook is some pampering for herself. Such a gift won't soon be forgotten.

Up for Discussion

To whom did your family choose to give a spa day? What was the response? How can a spa day help someone who's anxious to relax?

Read Phil. 4:6. Why do you think God tells us to not be anxious? What anxieties do you personally need to turn over to God?

1 Pet. 5:7 states, "Cast all your anxiety on him because he cares for you." Think about this verse. How can you give your anxieties to God? Why do you think God would want to carry the burden of everyone's anxieties?

Read Prov. 12:25. How is this verse true? In light of the other verses discussed, how can an anxious heart be avoided?

Do not be anxious about anything, but in everything, by prayer and petition, with thanksgiving, present your requests to God.
—Phil. 4:6

48. Plant a Garden

Do you know what the most popular vegetable is? Potatoes, of course! (Iceberg lettuce comes in second). Every American eats about 126 pounds of potatoes a year.[19]

Gather your family and plant a garden. Share its rewards—the healthful vegetables we all love—with your neighbors. Nothing says you love your neighbor like a basketful of homegrown tomatoes or ears of corn. Involve your children in every step of the process—from planting the seeds to harvesting the crops. Seek their assistance in watering, weeding, washing, and delivering the vegetables.

If other neighbors are willing, they might also enjoy planting their own gardens and then meeting at the end of the season for a neighborhood farmers market.

Another way to utilize the wholesomeness of a garden and share with others is to can the food. A friend of ours cans a variety of homegrown foods each year. Among them are chokecherries from her backyard, crab apples from a neighbor's yard, and cucumbers from a farmers market. She and her family can the food and then deliver the jars to family, friends, and church members, along with a loaf of homemade bread for the holidays. Their spicy pickled green beans have topped the list of favorites for those who enjoy hot flavors. Whenever they attend a potluck meal, they bring some of their famous canned jelly and leave it for the hosts. Canned and fresh goods make great housewarming gifts.

Whichever way you decide to utilize your garden, remember to instill in your children the amazing manner in which

God creates a tiny seed and from it grows wonderful foods to nourish and strengthen our bodies.

Up for Discussion

What vegetables or fruits did your family decide to grow in your garden? How were you involved with this project? Did your neighbors appreciate receiving a basket of the bounty? If your neighborhood came together and held a farmers market, how was this idea beneficial to all who participated? Were you able to give food to those who weren't able to join in the farmers market?

Read Gen. 1:29. Why do you think God created such a wide variety of fruits and vegetables?

Read and discuss the garden account in Gen. 3. The serpent persuaded Eve to eat from a tree that God had told her not to touch. Gen. 3:6 states, "When the woman saw that the fruit of the tree was good for food and pleasing to the eye, and also desirable for gaining wisdom, she took some and ate it. She also gave some to her husband, who was with her, and he ate it." What was the consequence of Eve's failure to listen to God's stern command? The serpent provided such a convincing line about why it was all right to eat from the tree that Eve believed him. How can you avoid temptation when it's directed at you in such a way that it seems all right to do it?

God said, "I give you every seed-bearing plant on the face of the whole earth and every tree that has fruit with seed in it. They will be yours for food."
—Gen. 1:29

49. Provide an After-School Alternative for a Latchkey Kid

Many children (8 percent, or 1.6 million five- to 14-year-olds) are "latchkey" kids—they spend some or all of their after-school hours home alone.[20]

Your family can invite a latchkey child to spend time at your home with your supervision after school. If this is not an option, invite your family to purchase a membership for the latchkey child at the local YMCA. The child will then have somewhere safe to go after school until his or her parents are home. There's no greater assistance your family can provide than to offer a safe haven for a child.

Up for Discussion

Discuss with your parents why it was important to offer your home to a latchkey child. If you chose to purchase a YMCA membership for a child, discuss how this will positively impact the child and his or her parents.

Read Luke 18:16-17. Why are children very important to Jesus? The Bible paints a delightful picture of Jesus and His kindness and listening ear toward children. Imagine how it must have been to gather at His feet, spend time with Him, and listen to Him speak. Discuss the safe haven He provides for us in heaven.

Jesus called the children to him and said, "Let the little children come to me, and do not hinder them, for the kingdom of God belongs to such as these. I tell you the truth, anyone who will not receive the kingdom of God like a little child will never enter it.
—Luke 18:16-17

50. Give a Handout

How often do we come across people who are having a bad day? How often do we wish we could give them a little something to cheer them up and make their day a little brighter? A good way to act on that desire is to purchase some chocolate candies (many people love chocolate!) to carry around with you. Chocolate square candies work the best. Tie a small ribbon on the candy (such as you would with a present). Have the candies on hand when you cross paths with someone who needs a pick-me-up. Hand the person one of the chocolate candies, and let him or her know you care and are praying for him or her. A lollipop with a Bible verse glued to the stick is also an option.

You know about Bible tracts—make a "treat tract"! It can be a great display of godly behavior. You can use the example found in the templates section to create a treat tract wrapper for a candy bar. Write kind words and/or a Bible verse, and draw pictures to decorate the jacket wrapper. Glue the long open side together to make a sleeve. Slip it onto the candy bar.

Below are some situations in which you may need to give a handout:

- A relative who's having a difficult time lately and could use a chocolate cheer-up.
- At a gathering place, such as a Bible study. I recall one time when I nearly bumped into a woman while heading down the hall at my women's Bible study. I could tell by the expression on her face that she was upset. Although I didn't know her, I wished I had a handout to offer her.

- Someone at school or work may need a handout. On those days when everything seems to go wrong, a handout is a must.
- Your children may encounter someone at school who didn't do well on a test.
- You may see an acquaintance while grocery shopping who could use a caring token.

Be sure to have a stash of handouts for those unexpected times when you and your family need to be the light in someone's dark day.

Up for Discussion

Read 1 Sam. 20:14. Why should we be imitators of the Lord's continual kindness? How can always having a handout on hand help with this goal?

Read 1 Sam. 25 about David and Abigail. Nabal, Abigail's husband, refused to offer food to David and his soldiers. When Abigail heard of this, she quickly prepared a meal for David and his men. How did her gracious food handout save many lives? How did it affect her future?

While a piece of chocolate or a lollipop won't likely save someone's life, it can affect the future of his or her day by adding a smile to it.

> Show me unfailing kindness like that of the LORD as long as I live.
> —1 Sam. 20:14

51. Sponsor a Child from Another Country

Several Christian agencies seek to bring the gospel to children in other countries One that helps people sponsor children is Compassion International. This ministry helps more than 950,000 children in more than 24 countries.[21] Invite your family to sponsor a child from another country.

Recently my parents decided to sponsor a little girl from Brazil. She comes from a poverty-stricken, single-parent home. My parents know they're making a difference in her life and are helping her attend school and learn about the God who created and loves her.

Have your children draw pictures and send photos and other fun, small gifts to your sponsored child. Many of the children write back, and your children may even gain a pen pal!

There are many other wonderful Christian organizations that assist children in foreign countries, such as Mission of Mercy. However, before deciding to donate to any charity, be sure to investigate them, either through the Better Business Bureau web site at <www.bbb.com> or the Evangelical Council for Financial Accountability at <www.ecfa.org>.

Up for Discussion

How can you become a youth spokesperson for impoverished children in your church and Sunday School and among your friends? How does knowing you're helping a real child who otherwise wouldn't have the basic necessities help you know you're making a difference? What can you do to help raise money for the monthly sponsorship? Do you feel this money is well spent? Why are your family's prayers for the child you sponsor critical?

Read 1 John 3:1. What does it mean to you to know that the child your family sponsors is a child of God? How do you personally know that God loves and cares for you? For the child your family sponsored?

> How great is the love the Father has lavished on us,
> that we should be called children of God!
> —1 John 3:1

52. Encourage a Laugh

Laughter is one of the best ways to make a difference in someone's life. Laughter makes us forget all else in our lives. To hear the sound of pure laughter is one of the best sounds our ears will ever hear.

Encourage a laugh. Ask your family to be on the lookout for clean, funny jokes or comics. These can be found online on Christian joke web sites and sometimes in newspapers or magazines. Also, jokes they hear that can be written down are another possibility. Does your six-year-old love knock-knock jokes? Do silly one-liners hold a special place in the heart of your four-year-old? Does your husband love that new Christian comic strip? Do you have several clean e-mailed jokes that could be used? When everyone has collected enough jokes, paste them into a notebook. Present your joke book to someone who needs a good laugh.

Up for Discussion

To whom did you choose to present your joke book? How did it help someone who was otherwise sad? Why do you think God created laughter within us?

What was your favorite joke you included in the joke book? Did you or anyone in your family make up any jokes?

Proverbs 15:13 states, "A happy heart makes the face cheerful." How can a happy heart improve all areas of someone's life? How can a good clean joke contribute to this endeavor? Why should we find our humor only in clean jokes?

He will yet fill your mouth with laughter and your lips with shouts of joy.
—Job 8:21

53. Have a Jammie Day

The *Merriam-Webster Collegiate Dictionary* defines pajamas as "1: loose lightweight trousers formerly much worn in the Near East 2: a loose usu. two-piece lightweight suit designed esp. for sleeping or lounging."[22]

There's just something about new pajamas that makes one feel special. Comfortable new pajamas (many of which come in a one-size-fit-all category) are perfect for the following:

- The new or expectant mom
- The person recovering from an illness
- Someone living in a colder part of the country.
- The homebound person.

Don't forget a fuzzy pair of socks with the jammies. For an added touch, throw in a box of hot chocolate!

Up for Discussion

Why would jammies be a nice gift for someone who's ill or is a new mother? Who else do you know that could benefit from this project?

In John 13 Jesus washed His disciples' feet. Ponder how this is just one act Jesus performed that showed how He loved those He cared about. If Jesus can wash the feet of others, which are often dirty, smelly, and ugly, shouldn't we be able to do things of a much lesser magnitude?

Read John 13:13-17. What do you think Jesus meant when He said, "I have set you an example that you should do as I have done for you" (v. 15)? Did He mean *only* to wash other peoples' feet, or was there more to His command?

What other benefits did the jammies in the above activity have other than to clothe someone? Can you think of other suggestions in this book that serve a dual purpose?

Now that I, your Lord and Teacher, have washed your feet,
you should also wash one another's feet.
—John 13:14

54. Volunteer as a Tutor

By age 17, only about 1 in 17 seventeen-year-olds can read and gain information from specialized text.[23]

Is your teenage daughter a whiz at math? Does your son know the ins and outs of geography? Does one of your children possess a gift for teaching? Why not encourage your older child to volunteer to tutor a younger child who's having a difficult time in school? Consult your local library to see if such a program exists, and if so, how to sign up for it. If such a program doesn't exist, ask if there's a need for one to be started. Parents with available time may also want to inquire about volunteering for an adult literacy program.

The gift of time to assist someone in his or her schoolwork can make a world of difference in the life of a youngster.

Up for Discussion

What were some fun activities you incorporated into teaching someone how to read? Do you think we sometimes take for granted the fact that we can read? How would not being able to read make someone's life more difficult? How can knowing how to read open up an exciting world of adventure? Do you believe reading is more rewarding than watching television or playing video games? Why or why not?

Read about Solomon in 1 Kings 4. God promised to give Solomon anything he asked for. Solomon asked for wisdom. God answered his request and blessed him with great wisdom. Now read James 1:5. God promises wisdom to anyone who asks for it. Why is wisdom important? Why do you think Solomon chose that over material items and riches? What would you have chosen if you were Solomon?

God gave Solomon wisdom and very great insight, and a breadth of understanding as measureless as the sand on the seashore.

—1 Kings 4:29

55. Make Beautiful Music

The words of "Joy to the World" were written by Isaac Watts, who originally published the hymn in 1719. "[The hymn] is written in Common Meter and was originally called *The Messiah's Coming and Kingdom*. The hymn is based on the last half of the 98th Psalm. Although this psalm is about the coming kingdom of Christ on earth, much application to the first coming of Christ can be made in the first three verses."[24]

Gather your family and a few willing relatives, neighbors, and friends to Christmas carol around town or around the neighborhood. Include the classics, such as "Joy to the World," "Silent Night," and "The First Noel." Be sure to check with businesses first, and invite those around to join in with you.

Hand out engraved pencils or other small tokens that state that the "reason for the season" is Christ. After caroling, invite everyone to meet at your house for some hot chocolate.

Up for Discussion

What places did your family choose to sing carols? What type of reception did you receive? Did you invite onlookers to join you?

Ephesians 5:19 states, "Speak to one another with psalms, hymns and spiritual songs. Sing and make music in your heart to the Lord." How is singing to the Lord a form of worship? If you have a talent for singing, how can you use it to glorify the Lord at other times of the year besides Christmas? Discuss how some singers in the secular world have been gifted with excellent singing voices. Instead of singing songs pleasing to the Lord, they've instead chosen to sing offensive songs. Why should the gifts God gives us be used in ways that glorify Him?

> Shout for joy to the Lord, all the earth. Worship the Lord with gladness;
> come before him with joyful songs.
> —Ps. 100:1-2

56. Share the Gospel

Want a creative way to spread God's Word? Design and make a scripture prayer book to distribute. Older children can write their favorite Bible verses, one to a page. Younger children can provide drawings for the cover and the interior. Your family may choose to use a spiral notebook or have several pages that each person has written bound together at your local office supply store. A loose-leaf binder also works well. Additional verses can then be periodically added. An artistic idea would be to punch holes on the left-hand side of each of the verse pages. Then attach them with colorful yarn.

Flip through God's Word to discover which verses you will use. Some suggestions:

- Ps. 80:3
- Prov. 4:23
- Micah 7:7
- Matt. 15:10
- Matt. 21:22
- John 3:16
- John 14:6
- Rom. 6:23
- Eph. 2:4
- Eph. 2:8-10
- 1 Thess. 5:16-18
- Heb. 12:2-3
- Phil. 4:8

If multiple books are needed, have your children write the verses, illustrate the pages, and then have copies made of each complete book at your office supply store. Our family designed scripture prayer books using small spiral notebooks. We took turns writing our favorite verses, and our daughters drew the illustrations, one per page. We mailed these as Christmas gifts to our Christian and unbelieving family members and friends.

This project makes excellent gifts. And not only is this a great witnessing tool, but it also can help the recipient (and your family as well) memorize Bible verses.

Up for Discussion

How many prayer books did your family make? To whom did you distribute them? Did you think of other clever ways to personalize the book? Why is a homemade prayer book more meaningful than a store-bought one? What are the benefits of such a book?

Why is John 3:16 a good verse to be included in your scripture prayer book?

Read Matt. 28:19-20. How can knowing that God is with you always encourage your faith? How can this encourage the one(s) to whom you give the scripture prayer book?

Why does God need disciples in every corner of the world? How can you be a disciple in your own hometown?

> Go and make disciples of all nations, baptizing them in the
> name of the Father and of the Son and of the Holy Spirit,
> and teaching them to obey everything I have commanded you.
> And surely I am with you always, to the very end of the age.
> —Matt. 28:19-20

57. Sew Blankets

Are you or anyone in your family handy with a needle or a sewing machine? Enlist grandparents to sew blankets for children in orphanages. With soft material such as fleece, a blanket can mean the difference between going cold or staying warm for a child. A friend of ours who regularly participates in this project uses flat sheets, stuffs them, and sews them together for added thickness.

This simple item, one that most of us take for granted, can truly make a difference. Check with your church for the name of an organization that can distribute these blankets to children abroad. There are also children's homes throughout the United States that could use the gift of a blanket. Another idea is to donate blankets to a hospital for the children's ward. The children can then take these blankets with them when they leave.

My oldest daughter, who has a heart for those less fortunate, told me the other day, "Mom, poor people are like flowers. If they're not cared for, they wilt and die." I thought about the truth of her words. If we don't water the flowers and make sure they're planted in good soil, they won't live. The same is true for those less fortunate, such as those in orphanages. If we don't care about them and provide things they need, even things as simple as blankets, they, too, will wilt and die.

Up for Discussion

How can those who deliver the blankets to the children in the orphanages use the blankets to explain God's love?

Brightly colored fabrics used for the above project can bring additional hope for those who receive them. Explain why this is true. If you have a talent of sewing, how else could you use this talent for God?

A warm blanket can mean the difference between life and death. How does God's love help us to survive even when times in our lives are difficult?

Read Deut. 10:18. Discuss how even though a child may not have parents, a widow may have lost her spouse, and the alien may be in a strange land, God loves him or her even if there's no one else on whom he or she can rely. Next time you're in the midst of a crowd of people, remember that God loves everyone and yearns for everyone to know Him.

> *He defends the cause of the fatherless and the widow,*
> *and loves the alien, giving him food and clothing.*
> —Deut. 10:18

58. Give Some Relief Time

Moms, especially new moms, are exhausted and may need a few minutes alone. Give a mom some relief time by offering to watch the children while Mommy—

- Takes a nap.
- Relaxes in a tub full of bubbles.
- Runs some errands (much easier without children to load and unload).
- Sit in the car while she takes one child in to a doctor's appointment.

Present a coupon to the mom, such as the one found in the templates section.

Up for Discussion

What was your role in helping a mother for the above activity? What do you think your family's participation in this project meant to her?

Read Isa. 66:13. When times are troublesome, why is it nice to know that God will console you, just as a mother comforts her child? How does the visual of God's arms wrapped around you in a hug providing consolation make the difficult times easier to bear?

Read Acts 10 about Cornelius, the Roman soldier, and his visit with Peter. Cornelius was praying when an angel appeared to him and told him to send for Peter. Cornelius did as he was told and was eager to hear what Peter had to say. Acts 10:34-35 states, "Then Peter began to speak: 'I now realize how true it is that God does not show favoritism but accepts men from every nation who fear him and do what is right."

Before this time, some believed that God sent His Son only for His chosen people. Now Peter and many others began to realize that God sent Jesus for all—both Jew and Gentile. Verse 43 states, "Everyone who believes in him receives forgiveness of sins through his name." Why is this story comforting? Why is it a relief that God shows no favoritism?

As a mother comforts her child, so will I comfort you
—Isa. 66:13

59. Plan a GTYC Day

Make a clothing donation by planning a GTYC (Go Through Your Closet) Day. Each member of the family goes through his or her closet to find any clothing that no longer fits or he or she no longer needs. Before washing the clothing, be sure it's free of holes and stains.

Set a goal for your family. A large box, two garbage sacks, or a laundry basket—whatever goal you use, attempt to fill it with clothing for someone who needs it.

Contact your church, the Salvation Army, Goodwill Industries, a homeless shelter, or a missions group to find out if they know of anyone in need of clothing. I recall one time a member of our church posted announcements that she had clothing and baby items from her boy/girl twins that she no longer needed and would be happy to donate it to anyone who needed it. Her children were toddlers, so the items were still up to date and in great condition. Sure enough, several people in the congregation were either expecting a baby or recently had a baby. What a blessing the items were to them!

What better way to clear the clutter in your home and help someone in need at the same time? Whether it's people re-entering the work force in need of clothes while seeking employment, those who have come on hard times, those who have recently had an addition to their family, people at a shelter, or people in third-world countries—if there are clothes to be given away, there's someone who needs them.

A bonus: when you've completed your GTYC Day, head to the nearest ice cream shop with your family for a double scoop of your favorite ice cream!

What charity did your family decide to help for the above project? What was your motivation? Did you meet your goal? Give several reasons a GTYC Day should occur each year.

Have you ever kept clothes you no longer needed, wanted, or hadn't worn in a long time? How could just one pair of jeans or a sweatshirt mean much more to someone who has nothing and be more useful than sitting in a pile of things that are never worn?

Read Matt. 25:36. Ponder how Jesus clothes us with His love.

> *I needed clothes and you clothed me.*
> —Matt. 25:36

60. Welcome New Neighbors

Whenever a new family moves into the neighborhood, design a "Welcome, Neighbor!" gift pack. Load a basket with the following:

- Homemade goodies—most people love homemade cookies or bread
- A Bible (inexpensive pocket-size New Testaments can sometimes be found at department stores)
- A list of area churches
- A list of area restaurants, grocery stores, parks, and playgrounds (if they have children)
- A card offering to watch their home while they're out of town.
- When you've finished packing it, join with your entire family (never send children alone) to deliver the basket.

This idea can also extend beyond your neighborhood. Why not fill a basket for that new family who recently began attending your church? Include information about Sunday School classes, youth group meetings, church missions, and children's programs.

No matter who you design the basket for, it's sure to be gladly received, because everyone likes to feel welcomed.

Up for Discussion

Why is getting along with your neighbors important? How can the above project help your neighbors feel welcomed? How can it develop the beginning of a positive relationship between your family and your new neighbors?

Have you and your family ever moved to a new neighborhood? Did you feel welcome? If so, what did those in the neighborhood do to make you feel welcome? If not, what could they have done to make your family feel more welcome?

If you chose also to make a gift basket for the new family at church, how do you think this made them feel like part of your church family? Why is it important to make someone feel welcome at church, especially a newcomer? How might a warm welcome affect the person's decision to return to your church? If a nonbeliever in search of God receives a kind welcome, how would his or her attitude be affected in attending a church and learning more about God?

Read John 10 about Jesus' role as our shepherd. Verse 11 states, "I am the good shepherd. The good shepherd lays down his life for the sheep." How is Jesus like a shepherd? How are we like sheep? How are those in your neighborhood like sheep?

Now read the parable of the lost sheep in Luke 15:1-7. Why would someone make the effort to find one lost sheep when he or she has 99 other sheep? How does this correlate to people who are lost, and Jesus in His role as the shepherd?

Read Prov. 27:10. How can having good neighbors make life much more pleasant?

> Better a neighbor nearby than a brother far away.
> —Prov. 27:10

61. Decorate with Love!

You don't have to have a creative flair or a home interior decorating degree to make a difference. Gather your family, and offer to decorate a nursing home, hospital, children's hospital, children's home, or homeless shelter. Obtain permission from the director to decorate the facility for a holiday, such as Christmas, or "just because." If you choose to decorate with no holiday in mind, explore different themes. Here are some ideas:

- Wild West theme—Gather 'round and use hats, ropes, saddles, and other cowboy paraphernalia to bring back the days of the Old West.
- Animal theme—This is a perfect theme for the children's home or children's hospital. Using stuffed animals, animal posters, and pictures your children have drawn and painted on large poster board, use this theme to celebrate some of God's cutest and cuddliest creatures.
- Flower theme—What a wonderful way to brighten the day! Using silk and paper flowers, and streamers, create a flower garden theme. Include your children in creating enormous flowers cut out of large pieces of construction paper and attached to the walls (with permission).
- Jungle theme—Life-sized stuffed leopards and snakes, along with leopard material can make for an exciting jungle theme for the children's home.
- Birthday theme—Enlist your children to wrap presents (small useful gifts, such as socks, hats, or a tablet and pen). Decorate with presents and balloons for a birthday theme. When it's time to take the theme down, pass out the presents to the residents.

- Book theme—Make copies of covers of top-quality books, and string them around for a book theme at the homeless shelter. Provide copies of books that may be of interest to be later used in the shelter library. Some ideas include *Every Day Deserves a Chance*, by Max Lucado; *Deliverance from Daily Giants: The Power to Conquer Worry, Fear, Failure, and Other Giants*, by Dwight M. Gunter II; *The Case for Christ*, by Lee Strobel; *Get Out of That Pit*, by Beth Moore; and *Life Is Just Better with Jesus*, by Ann Graham Lotz.

- 50s or 60s theme—Using paraphernalia from days past, create an atmosphere from a time when poodle skirts ruled, records were a must-have, and souped-up cars were the norm. Clothes from this era can be located at second-hand stores or in attics of older family and friends. Small replica cars from that era can be inexpensively purchased at toy stores. Write the titles of some of the top hits of those decades on homemade records cut out of black construction paper. Leave a stack of paper in a visible area, and encourage the residents to write about their fondest memory during that period.

Whatever theme you use, don't forget to do a follow-up. Perhaps this could become a family tradition—to use your creative minds and clever decorating skills to brighten the day of another!

Up for Discussion

Which theme did you and your family choose to use to decorate? Where did you decorate? What other themes can you add to the list? Why would a decorated atmosphere make a difference in someone's life?

Read 1 Kings 5—8 about Solomon building the Temple. Why did he go to so much trouble to build such a spectacular edifice? Describe some of the highlights of this worship place and some of the decorations used. What were some of the furnishings included in the Temple? 1 Kings 8 describes the ark of the covenant placed in the Temple. What is the ark of covenant, and why was it so important that it was placed in the Temple?

Read Eph. 6:11. What type of armor does Paul say to cover yourself with? How can decorating yourself with the "full armor of God" protect you? Read on to verse 13. How strong is this armor? Why does the strength of the armor provide reassurance?

> Put on the full armor of God so that you can take your
> stand against the devil's schemes.
> —Eph. 6:11

62. Remember Our Soldiers and Their Families

The humbling sign at a veterans' hospital states, "The Price of Freedom Is Seen Here." We in the United States are very fortunate to live in freedom, and we have the ones who have fought and continue to fight to thank for the privilege to live here.

Those who fought in prior wars for our freedom deserve our gratitude. Organize a celebration for veterans at your local nursing home or veterans' home. Contact the director for permission and the number of veterans who will be attending the celebration. Everyone in the nursing or veterans' home is invited. Below are some suggestions:

- Serve refreshments, such as red, white, and blue frosted cupcakes (in the United States) or cookies or a large sheet cake frosted with a flag of your country.
- Enlist your children to design a certificate for each veteran, thanking the veteran for what he or she has done (see the example found in the templates section).
- Sing "America the Beautiful" or "The Star Spangled Banner," and invite each one to join in the singing.
- Hand out small flags to everyone in attendance.
- Take photos of the veterans (with their permission, of course) to print later and hang in the dining area of the home where they will be remembered daily.
- Contact your local newspaper and ask if they would be interested in featuring some of the vets in an article honoring them.

Suggest that your town or city promote Veteran's Day, Memorial Day, or Independence Day by sponsoring a parade for each or all of these holidays. Invite all those who have fought or plan to fight for our country to be a part of the parade.

Suggest that your teenage son or daughter interview a veteran. The number of World War II veterans is quickly dwindling, which makes it all the more critical to have their stories written down before they're gone. Be sure to attend the interview with your teenager (it's never a good idea to send someone alone on an interview), and offer to help record the information. When I wrote a book a couple of years ago about people aged 70-90, I was privileged to interview several WWII veterans. Since that time, one has passed away, but the story he told me remains forever secured in print.

Another way to remember our soldiers is to recognize the ones who are fighting even today in the war on terror. Remember our women serving also. There are 203,000 active-duty women in the military as of September 30, 2005.[25] Many of them are in the midst of roadside bombs and other unsafe conditions. Involve your family or church group to pack a care package for a soldier. Obtain the name(s) of a soldier serving in another country from your church or National Guard office.

Our children's church class undertook such a project one Sunday. During class, each child folded a brightly-colored piece of construction paper in half. Then he or she decorated the card using markers, crayons, and stickers. The child wrote messages on the inside of the cards, such as

- God loves you
- Happy Easter (Other holiday greetings may be used depending on the time of year)
- Thank you for fighting for our freedom and the freedoms of others
- We appreciate you
- We're praying for you

- [Various Bible verses]

We contacted and asked the soldier's mother what else we could include in the package we were sending. Teary-eyed and grateful, she told us how her son loved beef jerky, licorice, and gum and how such items were not available where he was—a small camp in the middle of the desert in Iraq. We included these items, other non-perishable treats, and a card game in the package.

Your family can also make a difference by remembering and supporting the families of active military personnel. When a spouse is called to active duty, the parent at home takes on the role of both. Below are some things you can do to help the parent during this time of uncertainty:

- Offer to help deliver children to school and/or take them home.
- Offer to run errands or pick up some much-needed groceries.
- Promise to keep the family in your prayers and follow through with that promise.
- Call or e-mail on a weekly basis to see if there are other needs.

When a friend of ours learned her husband would be serving in Iraq for six months, our prayer group was quick to let her know that we were there for her. Sometimes just knowing that someone cares is the biggest comfort of all.

Up for Discussion

Which project(s) did your family undertake in the above activity? Why is it important to remember and honor our past and present members of the Armed Forces?

Discuss John 15:13. How are those who have fought in the past for our country and those fighting now giving up their lives for others? Why do you think this is an important verse, and how does it correlate to what Jesus did for us?

Read Judg. 6—7 about Gideon's calling and later his defeat of the Midianite army. Gideon, a farmer, was shocked and unsure when the Lord told him, "I will be with you, and you will strike down all the Midianites together" in Judg. 6:16. Gideon asked for signs that it was truly God speaking to him.

Once convinced, Gideon assembled an army, only to have it reduced to the size of only 300 men upon instructions from God. The Midianite army was large—in Judg. 7:12 the people were described "thick as locusts. Their camels could no more be counted than the sand on the seashore." Still, Gideon and his small army were able, with the Lord's help, to defeat the Midianites. Discuss how sometimes faith is all we have during difficult times and why it's the most important.

Read Rom. 8:31. How is this applicable in the story of Gideon? How was Gideon's faith increased by the conversation he overheard in Judg. 7:13 and later with his victory? How has God protected our country through the years?

Some of the soldiers fighting the war on terrorism are from backgrounds that have little in common with fighting with the armed forces. How can God use those with diverse backgrounds, such as He used Gideon, for any of His purposes? How might He use you for His greater plan?

Greater love has no one than this, that he lay down his life for his friends.
—John 15:13

63. Think of Your Own Family Members

Many times through the hustle and bustle of everyday life, our own family members need to be reminded of just how much we care for them. Encourage each member of your family to participate in some or all of the following activities:

- Prepare a favorite meal. On a regular basis, I allow each of our daughters to decide what they would like for dinner. It has become a tradition to offer "Your Choice Night," and it takes the burden off me deciding what to make! Ask older children to assist you in cooking a meal for the person who gets to decide.

- Develop a Backwards Day. Nothing is more fun in our house than when Backwards Day rolls around. It's the day we eat pancakes and eggs for dinner. We also eat dessert before dinner. A fun addition? Add a little bit of food coloring to your pancake batter. The first time I served up turquoise pancakes, the looks on my family's faces were priceless. You can also wear your clothes inside out and walk backward.

- Make Dad's favorite cookies—and deliver them! Our daughters love to help cook special treats for Dad, and together we deliver them to his place of employment. If Mom works outside the home, teenagers can supervise younger children and make Mom's favorite dessert for delivery.

- Play what they want to play. Ever so often, one member of our family gets to pick something he or she really wants to do. When it's my choice, I choose to have the family join me for a walk down the walking path. When it's my older daughter's choice, she chooses to play "horses" with her toy horses. Rotate through the family so that once a month someone gets to pick. The caveat? Everyone else in the family has to join in!

- Purchase little surprises for family members. When my brother was little, my sister and I made up the idea of "Mrs. Cookie." One night a week while our brother was sleeping, we left a surprise for him on the desk next to his bed. He awoke very excited to find a simple gift, such as a handful of pennies, a toy out of a gumball machine, or a treat bag. Have your older children partake in this activity for their younger sibling(s).

- Lend your favorite toy. I encourage our daughters to lend each other their favorite toy for an hour or so. This is a great way to teach the concept of sharing and the fact that there are more important things than a toy. My children especially love it when I lend them one of my special toys from when I was child.

- Read. Before my older daughter reads her favorite *Box Car Children* books, I ask that she please read her younger sister two books. My younger daughter, who can't yet read, chooses two of the books she would like to have read to her.

- Leave notes. My husband and I leave each other notes each day. I write his while making his lunch at night. He writes mine before he leaves for work in the morning (and long before I'm awake!) Leave notes in your children's lunch boxes. Have your children leave notes for each other and for their parents. The notes don't have to be long—just a line or two letting the recipient know how important he or she is to the one writing the note.

- Offer your assistance. Does Dad need help in that daunting task of cleaning the garage? Does Mom need help with the overwhelming loads of laundry? Does your second-grader need help with that art assignment? Is your fifth-grader struggling with his science project? Encourage your family to help each other out in times of need. Ask them to be diligent in noticing and asking each other if assistance is needed.

Up for Discussion

Which of the above were you able to do for your family members? Were you the recipient of any of the above activities? What other recommendations can you think of for your family? Why do we sometimes forget the people who share a home with us when it comes to doing nice things for others?

Discuss 1 Tim. 5:8. Paul is very clear that our family should come first. How can your family make every effort to put each other at the top of the list? Who should be the very first one on the list above all else? Why?

If anyone does not provide for his relatives, and especially for his immediate family, he has denied the faith and is worse than an unbeliever.

—1 Tim. 5:8

64. Create a Bike Ministry

Two Christmases ago, our family decided to undertake a new ministry. It quickly became my husband's passion, as he set aside time in his busy schedule to help less fortunate children in our community and form a bike ministry.

We called our local Salvation Army and asked if there was a need in the community for refurbished bicycles. The captain told us that many children of families they served had put a bike on their "wish list" for Christmas. She told us the ages of the children so we would know what size bike to refurbish. Our next step was to contact family and friends and ask for any used bicycles that they no longer needed. Before long, our garage was filled with bikes waiting for a new home. The Salvation Army graciously donated the remainder of the used bikes from their inventory to fill the need.

My husband sanded off the old paint, repainted the bikes in stylish colors and many times with awesome designs. (I think artistry is one of his talents!) He fixed tires, chains, and kickstands and replaced what parts needed replaced. Our daughters and I made a trip to purchase new bike baskets, horns, and other doodads that personalized each bike.

A few weeks before Christmas, we delivered the bikes to the Salvation Army. They delivered the bikes to children in our community who might otherwise never have known the joy of owning a bicycle.

Your family can make a difference in this way as well. Be sure to start well enough ahead of Christmas as refurbishing does take time. Enlist your children to help fix the bikes and purchase decorative items. What an excellent way for children to learn gratitude for how fortunate they are!

What was your role in this activity? What other items did your family include with each bike? How could a Christmas card tucked in the basket of the bike add a special touch? What would you write in the card? Is it hard for you to imagine a child wanting a bike yet having no means to obtain one?

1 Cor. 12:24-26 states,

> God has combined the members of the body and has given greater honor to the parts that lacked it, so that there should be no division in the body, but that its parts should have equal concern for each other. If one part suffers, every part suffers with it; if one part is honored, every part rejoices with it.

In this activity there's a role for everyone in your family. If someone doesn't find the bikes to refurbish, the project can't happen. If someone doesn't fix and paint the bike, the activity doesn't transpire. If someone doesn't buy "extras" and deliver the bikes, children in need of them will never receive them. Discuss how family teamwork was critical for this project. Ponder teamwork in correlation with 1 Cor. 12:24-26. Discuss this verse in relation to all the people in the world, in your community, in your church, and in your family. Why would it be important that there is concern for each member? What do the people in each of those scenarios have in common?

Read Ps. 145:8. Why is it to our benefit that God is "slow to anger and rich in love?" How would our lives be affected if the opposite were true, that God is quick to anger and without much love? How can we mirror God's ways and also be gracious, compassionate, patient, and loving, especially in areas of giving to others?

> The LORD is gracious and compassionate, slow to anger and rich in love.
> —Ps. 145:8

65. Extend an Invitation

Many people who don't have family nearby would love to be invited to your home for Thanksgiving or Christmas dinner or a summer picnic. Ask your church secretary or pastor for a few names of those who would love to be a member of your family if only for a dinner. Nursing homes and assisted living facilities can also provide names of residents who won't be having any visitors for the holidays. Many are very lonely and would enjoy being a part of your family.

If you choose to invite someone for Christmas, have your family pick out a special generic gift for that person. Also, find out what the person's favorite dinner item is and prepare it for him or her.

After the meal, be sure to ask if your guest would enjoy a to-go bag with some leftovers to enjoy the following day.

Years ago, our extended family invited a dear widow named Peggy to our Christmas dinner. Because she had macular degeneration and could no longer see well, we offered transportation from her assisted living home to my parents' home for the meal. We cooked her favorite dessert, reveled in her strong faith, and watched as she took great delight in holding the three grandbabies. Photographs were taken, and we strove to make sure she was comfortable, felt like a part of our family, and had an enjoyable time. Peggy has since gone home to be with the Lord, but the memories of spending time with someone so remarkable will be with us forever.

Up for Discussion

Think about how my family invited Peggy to our Christmas dinner. How must this have been more enjoyable for her than a group dinner at the assisted living home? Although Peggy was not poverty stricken, what might have been her needs, and how do you think our family could have filled them?

What did you learn from the person you invited to your family's dinner or picnic? How did the time spent with your family compare with where the person might have spent his or her afternoon or evening? What were the needs he or she may have had that your family was able to fill?

Read Rom. 12:13. What is hospitality, and why is it important? 1 Pet. 4:9 states, "Offer hospitality to one another without grumbling." How could complaining about sharing your home with someone who's alone for the holidays negate the joy of sharing with others?

Share with God's people who are in need. Practice hospitality.
—Rom. 12:13

66. Make Meals

When my sister had mononucleosis as an adult, some women in our church rallied together to make a month's worth of meals for her. As the mother of twin toddlers, she was especially grateful for the kindness of these women. Such a gesture can be a blessing.

Dig out the cookbook, pass out the aprons, and encourage your family to join you in preparing several freezable dishes for one of the following:

- The couple who just had a new baby and is adjusting to parenthood.
- The tired mother of young children. For such a person, pulling an entrée out of the freezer and popping it into the oven for dinner is more than a convenience—it's a sanity-saver.
- Someone suffering from an extended illness who may be too weak to make meals.
- Someone who has just experienced a death in the family and is unable to focus on preparing meals during his or her time of grief.
- A homebound individual or couple.

Give each of your family members a specific job. For older children, setting out the necessary ingredients, mixing the ingredients, or washing the dishes after preparing the meal is an option. For younger children, allow them to measure and pour the ingredients into the bowls (with supervision).

Below are some suggestions for this project:

- Provide instructions for cooking. Older children can write the stove temperature, baking time, and other details on a small recipe card to be given with the dish.

- Purchase disposable cooking dishes with lids so that when the family is done with their meal, they don't have to worry about washing and returning the dish.
- Provide side dishes, such as biscuits, cut-up veggies, washed grapes, or cut-up chunks of cantaloupe or watermelon.
- Include napkins and disposable silverware that can be conveniently tossed when the meal is over.
- Include a coupon with an offer for additional meals if needed.
- Remember that if you're making meals for an individual or couple to be sure the food portions aren't too large so food won't be wasted.

Remember to include your family in not only preparing the meals but also in the shopping for and delivering of meals. Remind your children early in their lives that God has called each one of us to serve.

Up for Discussion

Who did your family choose to help for this activity? How could something as simple as preparing a meal be a lifesaver for someone in need? Discuss how we take for granted the ease of preparing a quick dinner. For some, this task is not possible due to illness, time constraints, or financial reasons.

Read Exod. 16 about the story of how God provided manna and quail for the Israelites. Discuss how God took care of His people. How does He take care of you and your family? Why do you think it's necessary to help take care of others?

Read Prov. 22:9. What other verses can you find in the Bible that explain the importance of sharing what we have with others?

A generous man will himself be blessed, for he shares his food with the poor.
—Prov. 22:9

67. Provide Daily Inspiration and Encouragement

Know a family member or friend who could use some daily inspiration and encouragement?

Using various art supplies, enlist your children to help you decorate a large clean jar or plastic container with a lid. Have them handwrite or type in marker a label such as the one found in the templates section. Glue the label onto the middle of the jar.

Using colored index cards, ask your children to write on the papers kind thoughts and inspirations such as the following:

- I'm thinking about you today.
- God loves you.
- You're an important part of my life.
- Thank you for always being there for me.
- Thank you for being you.
- I'm thankful God placed you in my life.
- I'm thankful we're related [if a family member].
- You're like family to me [if a friend].
- I feel blessed knowing you.

Add any personal thought that makes that person special to you and your family.

Write as many inspirations as possible, preferably 30 (for an entire month). If necessary, thoughts may be repeated. When your children have written enough thoughts, fold the thoughts in half and drop them into the jar. Present it to a family member or friend. Depending on how many thoughts you've included in the jar, this gift will keep on giving for a month or more.

Up for Discussion

Were you able to think of any other thoughts to include in the jar? How could this gift be made in duplicate and presented to multiple people in need of a daily inspiration?

Read in 1 Sam. 19 about how Saul attempted to kill David. Although he promises his son, Jonathan, "As surely as the LORD lives, David will not be put to death" (v. 6), Saul continued to hunt David. In 1 Sam. 23, read about Saul's continual pursuit of David. How must David have felt when Saul relentlessly chased him with the goal of killing him? What hope did God provide for David? How did He keep David safe? Discuss how in 1 Sam. 24, in an interesting turn of events when later given the chance to kill Saul, David chose not to do so.

Throughout the book of Psalms, David discusses the encouragement he received from the Lord during the various trials of his life. How could your daily inspiration jar provide encouragement for those having a difficult time? What specific prayer could you pray for them? How does God comfort us through those times in our life that are most troubling to us?

> He lifted me out of the slimy pit, out of the mud and mire;
> he set my feet on a rock and gave me a firm place to stand.
>
> —Ps. 40:2

68. Host a Party

Want to make a difference in the life of a teenager?

"Every day, on average, 11,318 American youth (12 to 20 years of age) try alcohol for the first time, compared with 6,488 for marijuana; 2,786 for cocaine; and 386 for heroin."[26]

What better way to make a difference than to help curb the growing alcohol/drug use problem in our world? Partner with the preteens and teens in your family, and offer to host a youth group party at your house. Consider some of the following:

- Ask your computer-savvy teen to type up an invitation for the party. Be sure to specify that there will be no alcohol involved.
- There are many "cool" Christian rock bands—ask your children which groups they enjoy, and plan to play that music (or Christian videos) in the background.
- Decorate your home and/or patio area with colorful streamers.
- Go shopping with your children for party foods, such as, chips and salsa, mini-cupcakes, veggie plates, slices of watermelon, mini-ham and cheese sandwiches, potato salad, and soda. Be sure to purchase napkins, plates, cups, and plastic silverware as well. Attendees may even want to design their own sandwiches. In that case, provide ketchup, mustard, pickles, and lunch meats.
- Find a fun game or two for teens to play, such as Apples to Apples: Bible Edition.
- Own a ping-pong table, pool table, or foosball table? Put it to good use!

- Find a few inexpensive items to give as door prizes.
- Invite a few other parents to join you in chaperoning the party.
- Be available, but don't hover.

A few years ago my sister and her husband, then a high school teacher, threw a youth party. It was a huge success and was followed by another such party. Some of the teenagers were able to ask my brother-in-law tough questions about faith—ones that he was able to answer and help them on their path toward Jesus.

Your family can impact the lives of teens as well by inviting them to your home and being role models they can truly look up to.

Up for Discussion

What was the reaction to the party your family hosted? Do you plan to have more of these parties in the future? How was the party an excellent opportunity to live out your faith and to answer any questions your peers may have about God? Who can you direct your friends to if you don't know the answers? Did you invite only Christian friends? What would be a benefit of inviting someone who's not a Christian?

Discuss the importance of having alternatives to alcohol parties. Have you ever been to or been tempted to attend such a party? How can you resist the temptation to use alcohol and drugs?

1 Corinthians 6:19-20 states, "Do you not know that your body is a temple of the Holy Spirit, who is in you, whom you have received from God? You are not your own; you were bought at a price. Therefore honor God with your body." Discuss this verse and how critical it is that we view our bodies as the temples they are and take care of them in a manner pleasing to God.

Read James 1:13-15. How can a temptation that seems small and insignificant turn out to be bigger than expected? How can this temptation cause more trouble than first anticipated?

Discuss 1 Cor. 10:12-13. How is this verse comforting in light of the fact that in today's world there are so many temptations? What prayer can you pray asking God to protect you from temptation?

Ecclesiastes 12:1 states, "Remember your Creator in the days of your youth." Why is it important to attend youth events that teach and reinforce our Creator while you're young? How can this build a foundation for you as you grow older?

If you think you are standing firm, be careful that you don't fall! . . . And God is faithful; he will not let you be tempted beyond what you can bear. But when you are tempted, he will also provide a way out so that you can stand up under it.

—1 Cor. 10:12-13

69. Make a Run for It

Looking for a surprise way to make a difference this May Day? Why not celebrate it with a fun idea that requires tennis shoes?

Involve your children in decorating a brown paper bag, rolling down the top, and attaching a construction paper handle to make a vase. Before attaching the handle, write with markers a Bible verse such as "There is a time for everything, and a season for every activity under heaven" (Eccles. 3:1).

Help them make construction paper flowers with colorful petals glued to round craft stick stems, or purchase plastic or silk flowers and place them in Styrofoam. Place the flowers in the bag vase. On a round craft stick, make a construction paper flag with the words "Spring has sprung—enjoy your flowers!" This reminds your recipient of how wonderful it is that each spring is a chance to start anew.

With your children, put the vase of flowers on the porch of a neighbor or friend. Ring the doorbell, and watch from afar as the recipient discovers his or her surprise!

Up for Discussion

For this activity, what would be the benefit of using paper or silk flowers as opposed to real flowers?

Read Josh. 1:5. Fake flowers never die, just like God's love, which is unconditional. Ponder how knowledge of this verse is comforting. Although we can't count on family and friends to always be there for us, we can always count on the Lord. He will never change, and his love will never change, just as it states in Heb. 13:8—"Jesus Christ is the same yesterday and today and forever."

Read the story about Ruth's loyalty to Naomi in Ruth. Although she could have stayed with her family, she chose to follow her mother-in-law to a foreign country and worship God, as Naomi did, rather than the gods Ruth was accustomed to worshiping.

Ruth's fierce devotion led her into a relationship with the one *real* God. Just as God is faithful to us, Ruth was faithful to her mother-in-law, even if it meant leaving the home she knew. Is God loyal to us? Why should we be loyal to Him?

Ruth ultimately married Boaz and was the mother of Obed, who was the grandfather of David. The lineage continued to Jesus. Little did Ruth know that God would have chosen her for such an important plan.

I will never leave you nor forsake you.
—Josh. 1:5

70. Be a Job Scout

On any given day the classifieds section in your local newspaper is full of jobs waiting to be filled. Why not help someone you know who's unemployed find a job? A friend of our family who is a single mom was recently looking for a job. Since I received the newspaper, I happily forwarded it, complete with circles around jobs of interest for her. It wasn't long before she landed the "perfect" job. You can also learn of job openings through family and friends and forward the information to someone in need of a job.

Don't know anyone personally who needs a job? You can still make a difference. Each day make it a point to pray with your family that people searching for jobs will be matched with the right jobs in the classifieds and elsewhere. Pray that those employers searching for employees will find the ones who will be a perfect fit for their companies.

Up for Discussion

If you're in the process of completing the second half of this activity, how do you know that your prayers are being answered? Why should you exercise persistence and not give up even if you don't see any results? Why is praying for someone you don't know just as important as praying for someone you do know? How might a stranger react to the fact that someone unknown is praying for him or her?

Discuss the astonishing way that ants work together as a team to accomplish goals. They work hard to build homes, carry food much bigger than themselves, and take care of the young ants. How could we humans learn a thing or two from ants? Discuss how your family as a team can help someone find a job.

Read Mark 1:14-20. As Jesus proclaimed the Good News, He found Simon and Andrew fishing in the Sea of Galilee. In Mark 1:17-18 we read, "'Come, follow me,' Jesus said, 'and I will make you fishers of men.' At once they left their nets and followed him." Later, in verses 19-20, Jesus called to James and John to follow Him, and they, too, left without delay to follow their Savior. Jesus knew that these two men, among 10 others, would be His disciples. He knew the jobs they were to have for the Kingdom. Discuss how Jesus has a plan and a job for your life. How can you be sure you follow that plan?

But to put their hope in God, who richly provides us with everything.
—1 Tim. 6:17

71. Provide Gift Packs

Every day people everywhere are admitted to the hospital for serious illnesses and diseases. A small act of thoughtfulness can console those who are recovering.

"2004 statistics for the United States show that coronary heart disease (CHD) is the single leading cause of death in America. CHD causes heart attack and angina. . . . Estimates are that 9,100,000 people in the United States suffer from angina."[27]

Join your family in shopping for lotions, books (used books can be found inexpensively at thrift stores, garage sales, or library fundraisers), magazines, socks, generic pajamas, and small knickknacks. Put together small decorated boxes of items for those who are in the intensive care unit at the hospital. Place a piece of clear cellophane wrap around each box, and curl ribbons or add a bow for a cheerful look. Remember to include a generic card and a Bible.

Those who have suffered heart attacks, strokes, or other life-threatening circumstances will appreciate the thoughtfulness that comes with the boxes your family donates. The hospital will be able to have them on hand for when such needs arise.

Up for Discussion

What did your family write in the card that was included in the boxes you donated? What other words of comfort or verses would be especially helpful to someone facing any type of illness or disease? What other items did you place in the boxes? Why would decorating the boxes and adding the cellophane wrap and bows be important? How did completing this project humble you in regard to your own good health?

Proverbs 15:30 states, "Good news gives health to the bones." How could the boxes you provided be a form of "good news"? How would this apply to the good news in the Bible that was placed inside the gift packs?

Read Heb. 13:2. Discuss how this verse applies to the activities throughout this book that are done for strangers. Why should we think not only of family and friends when it comes to being thoughtful but also those we don't know?

> *Do not forget to entertain strangers, for by so doing*
> *some people have entertained angels without knowing it.*
> —Heb. 13:2

72. Furnish Winter Clothing

Enlist you family in making scarves for children in overseas orphanages or for those in children's homes in your own country.

My older daughter's class at school joined in making scarves for children in orphanages in Romania. The task was a simple yet important one. They took strips of colorful fuzzy fleece fabric that had been premeasured and cut to the proper length of a scarf. The scarves had been snipped at each end with several two-inch strips. The children tied the strips two at a time together into double knots. When they were finished, they had numerous scarves that would be delivered to children, some of whom lived on the streets during the cold winters. My daughter's class included homemade cards for the children to let them know that they were praying for and thinking about them.

When the missionaries delivered the homemade scarves, they took photos of the children with the scarves and the pictures my daughter's class had drawn. Seeing the photos with the children wearing the scarves and holding the drawings, my daughter and her classmates were able to realize the impact they made on children an ocean away.

Not only can these children (and needy children in your own town) use scarves, but they can also use hats, gloves, and gently used winter coats. Some cities organize coat drives, especially around Christmastime. When I looked through my daughters' closets, I was shocked to see how many coats they had. Hanging in the closet, the extra coats were worthless. Given to a needy child, the coats became valuable.

Such a project teaches children that not everyone has the luxury of a warm coat and gloves when it's cold outside.

Up for Discussion

My daughter's classmates were able to see the photos of the children they helped. Even if your family is not able to see the specific children you helped with this project, how do you know you still made a difference?

Read Matt. 6:4. Why does Jesus command us to keep our giving a secret? What would be wrong with telling others about what we have done? When if ever might it be all right to tell others?

> So that your giving may be in secret. Then your Father,
> who sees what is done in secret, will reward you.
>
> —Matt. 6:4

73. Host a Block Party

There's nothing quite like a hot summer night and a good barbecued hamburger. Why not celebrate the gift of summer with a neighborhood block party? Discuss the matter with your family, and involve them in making homemade invitations such as the one found in the templates section.

So many times life moves so quickly that we fail to greet, let alone truly meet, our neighbors. God's command in the Bible is to love your neighbors. How can we love them if we don't even know them? A block party is an excellent way to get to know those who share your neighborhood.

You may even decide to plan a game for the children, such as shooting some hoops at a freestanding basketball net or a game of croquet in the front yard. Sidewalk chalk drawings are also a good way to keep little hands busy. Plan to provide something to drink—this helps avoid the problem of alcohol being brought to the barbecue. Lemonade, ice water, iced tea, or two-liter bottles of soda are all suggestions. If you or some of your neighbors have picnic tables or plastic chairs, set these up, as well as a table for the food and condiments.

One of our neighbors has a movie projector that he likes to use in the cool summer evenings. If you or one of your neighbors has access to a projector, why not include this at the end of the block party? Be sure to pick a family-friendly movie (for suggestions, see activity 31).

Whatever you decide to include in your block party, make it clear that everyone in the neighborhood is welcome. Who knows? You might make new friends—you already have one thing in common—you use the same road to reach your homes.

How did hosting a block party help your family become better acquainted with your neighbors? Why would choosing a family-friendly film that's not displeasing to God be an important aspect of your block party? How might your family be the only witness for Christ some of your neighbors see?

Read Rom. 12:16. What's important about living in harmony with each other? How can the opposite result in unpleasantness in the neighborhood? Someone once said that you can't choose your neighbors. If you have less-than-kind neighbors, how can you get along with them as God commands? How would the following prayer be helpful?

Dear Father, I thank you for our neighborhood and those who live near to us. Please help our family to repair the discord that has occurred between our neighbors, the _____ family, and our family. They're difficult to love, Lord, but I pray that you'll help us to focus on their good qualities and to have the heart of Christ when dealing with them. Please soften our hearts so that we may live in harmony as you have commanded. In Jesus' name I pray. Amen.

Live in harmony with one another.
—Rom. 12:16

74. Make Your Voice Count

Is there a cause that is close to your family's heart? Protecting the unborn? Joining in the National Day of Prayer? Making sure our country remains free by allowing the right to exhibit the Ten Commandments? Protecting our children in the fight against violence in today's media? Involve your family in making their voices count for a good cause.

Last year my daughters and I joined in the pro-life moment of silence in front of our local courthouse. The cause was a respectful yet important one. We joined others in prayer for the many babies who never had a chance to be born, to be loved, or to go to school. We prayed for those who have had abortions, that God would heal their hearts. And we prayed for those who were contemplating abortions, that they would choose adoption instead. I explained to my children Ps. 139:13-14, which states, "You created my inmost being; you knit me together in my mother's womb. I praise you because I am fearfully and wonderfully made."

Whatever cause is close to your family's heart, be sure to explain to your children why it's important to respectfully protest those things that go against God's Word and how one voice does make a difference.

Up for Discussion

What cause did your family take a stand for in this project? Why do you think God wants us to stand up against unrighteousness? If the thought of doing so is terrifying, what prayer could you pray asking for God's strength in such a circumstance? Ps. 41:1-3 talks of God's protection. How is this helpful when you find yourself in the midst of having to fight for what's right according to God's Word? What would happen if no one voiced his or her opinion against pornography or violence in the media?

Read in 1 Sam. 1 the story of Hannah's sadness at not being able to have a child. God ultimately blessed her with Samuel, who would later become one of God's prophets. How might the gift of a child from a woman who chooses adoption instead of abortion bless a couple who would otherwise be unable to have children?

To prepare God's people for works of service, so that the body of Christ may be built up until we all reach unity in the faith and in the knowledge of the Son of God and become mature, attaining to the whole measure of the fullness of Christ.
—Eph. 4:12-13

75. Share a Story

Reading and sharing the written word with others can be a simple yet important thing. And all it will cost you is a little bit of your time. Below are some ideas:

- Many libraries offer story time for toddlers and pre-schoolers. Why not encourage your teenager who loves children to offer to read at the library during story time? He or she may also be able to assist the librarian with the craft that sometimes accompanies the story.

- Involve your family in organizing projects for children to partake in when they meet at the library after school. Suggestions might include a book-reading contest or an art contest in which those who visit the library vote for their favorite piece of art drawn by children who are a part of the after-school library program.

- Why not donate time to listen to children read at school? There's nothing quite like listening to little voices just learning to read. Some schools offer programs that allow teenagers to be aides and listen to elementary students learning to read.

- For teens who enjoy reading and helping others, a trip to a home for disabled children where your teen could read them a story and spend time with them is a blessing to both the giver and the receiver.

- Encourage your younger child who is an avid reader to take the time to help someone who is struggling with reading. A seven-year-old who is an accelerated reader can sometimes offer just the right motivation, suggestion, or helpful hint to his or her peer.

- Ask your older child to read to your preschooler or toddler. Children develop a love of reading from being read to on a regular basis.

Up for Discussion

Can you think of any other projects that involve reading that you could do? Think for a moment about the many parables Jesus told in the New Testament. Why was it important that He share these stories? How was He able to tell them in a way that made it easier for His listeners to understand? How can you read stories in a way that would make it easier for your listeners to understand?

Read Acts 8:26-40. Philip aided the Ethiopian man in understanding some significant points about Scripture. Had Philip not assisted him, the Ethiopian would have been hungry for the gospel yet never had his hunger satisfied with the answers to the questions he had.

Explain how a young child who may not hear stories often could depend on you to take him or her on an adventure as only books can.

Be imitators of God, therefore, as dearly loved children and live a life of love,
just as Christ loved us and gave himself up for us as a fragrant offering
and sacrifice to God.
—Eph. 5:1-2

76. Make It a Birthday to Remember

Ask your family to help you make someone's birthday one to remember. Each day for a month preceding the big day, mail something to the person having the birthday. Some ideas:

- A drawing of the recipient, drawn by you or a member of your family
- A favorite hard candy treat or pack of bubble gum
- A silly card
- A small gift book, such as one by artist Thomas Kinkade
- A magazine or newspaper article of interest to the recipient
- A photo of your family
- A handwritten Bible verse
- A favorite recipe
- Special candles that remain lighted even after attempts to blow them out
- A beautifully painted rock
- A card game
- A handwritten fond memory of the recipient

Be sure to be diligent in mailing something each day so that not a day goes by that the recipient doesn't receive something as his or her birthday nears. You may even wish to include something more significant for when the big day arrives!

Up for Discussion

Who did you decide would be the recipient in this activity? What type of response did you receive? What other items did you include during the days preceding the birthday? Discuss how this is a project that can be used for any age person. How would you modify it for someone who's 6? Someone who's 17? For someone who's 89?

Read Ps. 118:24. Why is every day something in which we should rejoice?

> *This is the day the* LORD *has made; let us rejoice and be glad in it.*
>
> —Ps. 118:24

77. Perform a Random Act of Kindness

Unfortunately, too often we hear of the bad things that take place in our world today. However, there are many nice things that happen every day due to someone choosing to love his or her neighbor. Your family, too, can join in performing a "random" act of kindness. Some suggestions:

- Put a shopping cart back for a mother. If you see a mother of young children unloading her cart in the parking lot of the grocery store, ask her if you could put her cart away when she is finished.

- Help someone carry out his or her groceries. Whereas it once was commonplace, in today's society many grocery stores don't have "bag boys" to assist people with their groceries. If you see an elderly person, someone who's disabled, or a mother with several children, offer to help carry his or her groceries to the car. It's a guarantee you'll be appreciated.

- Help someone who has "lost his or her load." One time when I was attempting to maneuver a cart completely full of groceries and children (and carrying two bags of groceries besides pushing the overloaded cart), I lost a watermelon. As I watched the oblong fruit roll down the sidewalk in front of me, I wondered how I would be able to retrieve it. Fortunately, a kind gentleman picked it up and placed it safely back onto my crowded cart. If you see someone who has lost a grocery item or two, offer to retrieve it for him or her.

- Hold the door open for someone, and let him or her go first.

- Give someone else the close parking spot. How many

times have you witnessed the scenario of two vehicles racing to a good parking spot? Why not let the other person have it? A little walk and a little fresh air are good for you!

- Place jars at businesses throughout town to raise money for people suffering from illnesses.
- Let someone in front of you in traffic, or let him or her go first at a four-way stop.
- If you have long hair and are planning to cut it, why not consider Locks of Love and donate your no-longer-needed hair to help a child who is suffering from long-term medical hair loss?[28]
- Send an anonymous donation. Check the newspapers for someone who was recently diagnosed with a serious medical condition, or for a family who recently lost their home to a fire. For someone with a medical illness and rising medical bills, financial assistance is sure to be a blessing. Such contributions are usually sent in care of a bank and are forwarded, to be used directly for the stated need.
- Be a grocery store gift-giver. Next time you are in the grocery store, think of the person behind you. What a nice surprise for the person when he or she approaches the grocery check-out counter and learns that someone has already paid for his or her groceries! This can be easily done by asking the cashier to add the groceries of the person behind you onto your tab. There's something especially heartwarming about doing something nice for someone you don't even know.

Include your own ideas for random acts of kindness below.

- _____

- _____
- _____
- _____
- _____

Up for Discussion

What items did you and your family undertake this week for this activity? How do you believe it made a difference, no matter how small?

Read the story about the Good Samaritan in Luke 10:25-37. Discuss how the Samaritan was performing a random act of kindness. It could have been anyone who traveled along the road from Jerusalem to Jericho on that day. There could have been additional people who acted toward the wounded man as did the priest and the Levite. Instead, it was a common man, a Samaritan, who came upon an injured man who had been beaten and robbed. The Samaritan, who may have been more likely than the others to ignore the injured man, instead assisted him. He provided an act of compassion that probably saved the man's life. Ponder why we should all try to be as the Samaritan was—eager to assist those in need no matter how different from us they may be.

Be kind and compassionate to one another, forgiving each other,
just as in Christ God forgave you.
—Eph. 4:32

Templates

10. Plan a Birthday Party

BIRTHDAY PARTY
HONORARY MEMBER

Name: _____

Actual Birthday Month: _____

Date of Party: _____

Member Since: _____

Happy Birthday to you!

We honor you and thank God for you
on your special day!

For you created my inmost being; you knit me together in my
mother's womb. I praise you because I am fearfully and
wonderfully made.
—Ps. 139:13-14

---

14. Invite and Deliver!

INVITATION

You are cordially invited to accompany our family to the (name of church here) this Sunday, _____ (date).

Time of pickup at your home: _____

Time of arrival at church: _____

Time church concludes: _____

RSVP: _____

We look forward to worshiping the Lord with you!

Signed: The _____ Family

*On this rock I will build my church,
and the gates of Hades will not overcome it.*
—Matt. 16:18

24. File Adoption Papers

ADOPTION CERTIFICATE

This certificate hereby certifies that
_____ is now an adopted
member of the _____ family.

Signed and dated this _____ day of
_____, 20_____, by the following
family members: _____,
_____, _____,
and _____.

Welcome to our family!

---

26. Remember Your Sisters and Brothers in Christ

38. Create a Movie or Game Night

MOVIE NIGHT TICKET

This entitles _____ to gather 'round for a family movie night, courtesy of the _____ family. Conditions of this ticket are that you must have fun and must be a member of the _____ family!

---

39. Pray Without Ceasing

41. Celebrate the Christmas Season

Calling all actors, singers, narrators, seamstresses, directors, prop builders, bakers, clean-up crews, makeup artists . . .

Sign up for the First Annual Church Christmas Program, to be held December 14.

Please write your name, contact information, and area of interest below.

Name	Phone number/ e-mail address	Area of interest

For more information, call _____.

Please sign up by _____ as the first meeting will be held on _____.

Let's make our Christmas program a success!

47. Plan a Spa Day

SPA DAY COUPON

This entitles _____ to
a special spa day. During such day, you will be pampered and treated to the following, all courtesy of the
_____ family:

A facial while you listen to soothing music,
A manicure and pedicure,
A new hairdo,
A cup of your favorite hot chocolate,
A relaxing snack with one of your favorite families.

Please call _____ for an
appointment.

We look forward to pampering you!

The small print:
To validate this coupon, recipient must enjoy being pampered.
Coupon is nontransferable.
Offer expires June 22, 2040

50. Give a Handout

To create a treat tract, use the following template:

Just wanted to let you know I was thinking about you today.

Hope you have a blessed and God-filled day!

This is the day the Lord has made;

let us rejoice and be glad in it.

—Ps. 118:24

- Fold here -

---

58. Give Some Relief Time

COUPON

This coupon is presented to _____
for three hours of "mommy time." Feel free to use
this time for pampering, errands, or relaxation.

Presented by _____.

---

62. Remember Our Soldiers and Their Families

CERTIFICATE OF THANKS

Today we honor you for the role you played in keeping our great country free. It is to you that we owe many thanks for the freedoms we enjoy every day. Know that we will never forget your sacrifices and courage. May we be reminded each and every day of your service to our country. God bless you!

Dated this _____ day of _____, 20____.

_____
Signature

_____
Signature

Greater love has no one than this,
that he lay down his life for his friends.
—John 15:13

67. Provide Daily Inspiration and Encouragement

DAILY INSPIRATIONS AND ENCOURAGEMENT

Made especially for _____

By _____

Directions: Open the jar and carefully remove one inspiration each day. As you do so, know that you are loved and cherished.

---

73. Host a Block Party

> ### YOU'RE INVITED
>
> The _____ (street, lane, avenue) neighborhood invites you to a neighborhood block party. Come meet and greet your neighbors!
>
> Bring your BBQ and plan to meet in front of the _____ residence. Please bring your choice of meat to grill for each family member, and a salad, dessert, or chips to share. Drinks will be provided.
>
> Please RSVP at _____ (phone number) by _____ (date).
>
> *We hope to see you there!*

Notes

1. U.S. Census Bureau, "Facts for Features," <http://www.census.gov/Press-Release/www/releases/archives/facts_for_features_special_editions/005870.html>.

2. Holiday Insights, "Bizarre and Unique Holidays," <http://holidayinsights.com/moreholidays/index.htm>.

3. U.S. Census Bureau, "The 65 Years and Over Population: 2000," Table 8, <http://www.census.gov/prod/2001pubs/c2kbr01-10.pdf>.

4. Mission Frontiers Magazine, "The State of World Evangelism," <http://www.missionfrontiers.org/newslinks/statewe.htm>.

5. The Humane Society of the United States, "Common Questions about Animal Shelters and Animal Control," <http://www.hsus.org/pets/animal shelters/common questions about animal shelters and animal control.html 3>.

6. Guinness World Records, <http://www.guinnessworldrecords.com/records/amazing_feats/teamwork/most_snow_angels_-_multiple_venue.aspx>.

7. MOPS, <http://www.mops.org/page.ph?pageid=84&srctype=menu>.

8. U.S. Census Bureau, "Census Bureau Projects Population of 300.9 Million on New Year's Day," <http://www.census.gov/Press-Release/www/releases/archives/population/007996.html>.

9. Safe Kids USA, "Injury Facts," <http://www.usa.safekids.org/tier3_cd.cfm?folder id=540&content item id=1030>.

10. *Merriam-Webster's Collegiate Dictionary*, 11th ed., s.v. "adopt."

11. Samaritan's Purse, "Operation Christmas Child: Volunteer," <http://www.samaritanspurse.org/OCC_Volunteer_Index.asp>.

12. American Speech-Language-Hearing Association, "Noise and Hearing Loss," <http://www.asha.org/public/hearing/disorders/noise.htm>.

13. Guinness World Records, <http://www.guinnessworldrecords.com/records/natural_world/plant_world/tallest_rose_bush.aspx>.

14. Mayo Clinic, "Walking for fitness: How to trim your waistline, improve your health," <http://www.mayoclinic.com/health/walking/HQ01612>.

15. Answers in Genesis, "A Tip on Tips," <http://www.answersingenesis.org/articles/am/v1/n1/tip-on-tips>.

16. U.S. Census Bureau, "Facts for Features," <http://www.census.gov/Press-Releaae/www/releases/archives/facts_for_features_special_editions/004109.html>.

17. Vision Beyond Borders, "VBB History," <http://vbbonline.org/pages/about/history.html>.

18. JoyofBaking.com, "Baking History," <http://www.joyofbaking.com/History.html>.

19. Iowa Department of Public Health, "February—Featured Vegetable: Potato," <http://www.idph.state.ia.us/Pickabettersnack/common/pdf/factsheets/potatoes.pdf>.

20. U.S. Census Bureau, "Bureau of the Census Statistical Brief," <http://www.census.gov/apsd/www/statbrief/sb94_5.pdf>.

21. Compassion International, "About Us," <http://www.compassion.com/about/aboutus.htm>.

22. *Merriam-Webster's Collegiate Dictionary*, 11th ed., s.v. "pajamas."

23. National Institute for Literacy, "Reading Facts," <http://www.nifl.gov/nifl/facts/reading_facts.html>.

24. Learn the Bible, "Joy to the World," <http://www.learnthebible.org/Joy%20to%20the%20World.htm>.

25. U.S. Census Bureau, "Facts for Features," <http://www.census.gov/Press-Release/www/releases/archives/facts_for_features_special_editions/009383.html>.

26. The Marin Institute, "Alcohol and Youth Facts," <http://www.marininstitute.org/Youth/alcohol_youth.htm>.

27. American Heart Association, "Heart Attack and Angina Statistics," <http://www.americanheart.org/presenter.jhtml?identifier=4591>.

28. Locks of Love, "What Is Locks of Love?" <http://www.locksoflove.org>.